COMPLETE CHET ATKINS GUITAR METHOD

Written By Chet Atkins

Edited, Revised, & Expanded by Tommy Flint

Cover guitar: Gibson Chet Atkins' Country Gentleman guitar
courtesy of Gibson Guitar Company, Nashville, Tennessee.

www.melbay.com/93232BCDEB

AUDIO CONTENTS

1 Tuning the Guitar (1:52)
2 The Six Five Jive (:45)
3 Yankee Doodle (:31)
4 Right Hand Development Alpha (1:02)
5 A Picking Study (:32)
6 Right Hand Etude (:33)
7 Home, Home, Can I Forget Thee (:59)
8 Remembering Home (:29)
9 Lightly Row (:48)
10 Long, Long, Ago (1:10)
11 The Marine Hymn (1:08)
12 Martha (1:22)
13 Tiptoe (:40)
14 Our Boys Will Shine Tonight (:35)
15 The Caissons Go Rolling Along (:58)
16 The Blue Tail Fly (:37)
17 Bicycle Built for Two (:48)
18 Oh, My Darling Clementine (:36)
19 My Mountain Home (:50)
20 Etude (:36)
21 The Wayfarin' Stranger (1:09)
22 America the Beautiful (0:00)
23 Three in One (:40)
24 Old Folks at Home (1:00)
25 Home on the Range (1:14)
26 Red River Valley (:51)
27 Waltz in E Minor (1:09)
28 May (:39)
29 March Majestic (1:03)
30 Prelude (:34)
31 Prelude in D Minor (:36)
32 Mist in the Valley (:38)
33 The Streets of Loredo (:46)
34 Smokey Mountain Lullaby (:46)
35 Drink to Me Only with Thine Eyes (1:27)
36 Etude in B Minor (:39)
37 Southern Picking (:20)
38 Love song (:58)
39 Etude in "D" (:39)
40 The Carnival of Venice (:32)
41 G String Etude (:21)
42 Smooth (:21)
43 Tenting Tonight (1:11)
44 Careless Love (:35)
45 Ode to Bob (1:15)
46 Chopin's Prelude (:47)

1 2 3 4 5 6 7 8 9 0

Visit us on the Web at www.melbay.com — E-mail us at email@melbay.com

Contents

Tuning the Guitar . . . 5
Another Method of Tuning . . . 6
Pitch Pipes . . . 6
Electronic Tuners . . . 6
The Rudiments of Music . . . 7
The Staff . . . 7
The Clef . . . 7
Notes . . . 8
Note Values . . . 8
Rests . . . 9
Notes and Comparative Rests . . . 9
The Time Signature . . . 9
Ledger Lines . . . 10
The Fingerboard . . . 10
Charts . . . 10
The Correct Way to Hold the Guitar . . . 11
Tablature . . . 12
The Fingerboard . . . 12
The Notes on the Sixth String (E) . . . 13
The Notes on the Fifth String (A) . . . 14
Whole-Notes . . . 14
Half-Notes . . . 14
Quarter-Notes . . . 14
The Notes on the Fourth String (D) . . . 15
Whole-Notes . . . 15
Half-Notes . . . 15
Quarter-Notes . . . 15
The Notes on the E ⑥, A ⑤, and D ④ Strings . . . 16
The Six Five Jive . . . 16
Yankee Doodle . . . 16
How Can I Leave Thee . . . 17
The Notes on the Third String (G) . . . 18
A Study on the Third String . . . 18
Lightly Row . . . 18
Running the Basses . . . 18
The Notes on the Second String (B) . . . 19
Whole-Notes . . . 19
Half-Notes . . . 19
Quarter-Notes . . . 19
The Notes on the First String (E) . . . 20
Three-Four Time . . . 20
Dotted Half-Notes . . . 20
Colonial Waltz . . . 20
Right Hand Development . . . 21
Alpha . . . 21
Two String Harmony . . . 22
A Picking Study . . . 22
Pick Up Notes . . . 22
Two and One . . . 22
Tone . . . 23
Tempo . . . 23
The Tie . . . 23
First and Second Endings . . . 23
Chromatics . . . 24
The Sharp . . . 24
The Flat . . . 24
The Natural . . . 24
Accidentally On Purpose . . . 24
Music in Two Parts . . . 25
Right Hand Etude . . . 25
Fingerstyle Etude . . . 25
The Key of C . . . 26
The C Scale . . . 26
Chords in the Key of C . . . 26
3/4 Accompaniment Style . . . 26
4/4 Accompaniment . . . 26
Home, Home, Can I Forget Thee . . . 27
Remembering Home . . . 27
Alternate Basses . . . 28
With Melody Notes . . . 28
Lightly Row . . . 29
Long, Long Ago . . . 30
The Marine Hymn . . . 31
Martha . . . 32
The Eighth Note . . . 33
Eighth Notes and Eighth Rests . . . 33
The Scale in Eighth Notes . . . 33
A Scale Study . . . 33
An Eighth Note Study . . . 34
Tiptoe . . . 34
Our Boys Will Shine Tonight . . . 35
The Caissons Go Rolling Along . . . 36
The Blue Tail Fly . . . 37
Bicycle Built for Two . . . 38
Oh, My Darling Clementine . . . 39
My Mountain Home . . . 40
Two-Four Time . . . 41
The Key of A Minor . . . 41
The A Minor Scale (Harmonic) . . . 41
Melodic . . . 41
The Chords in the Key of A Minor . . . 41
Etude . . . 42

A Minor Study 42
The Wayfarin' Stranger 43
Dotted Quarter Notes 44
America the Beautiful 44
How to Count Triplets 45
Triplets 45
The Key of G 46
The G Scale 46
A Scale Study 46
Three in One 47
Chords in the Key of G 48
Accompaniment Styles in the Key of G 48
Old Folks at Home 48
Home on the Range 50
Red River Valley 51
The Key of E Minor (Relative to G Major) 52
Two E Minor Scales 52
The Chords in the Key of E Minor 52
Accompaniment Styles in the Key of E Minor 52
Waltz in E Minor 53
The Key of F 54
The F Major Scale (Two Octaves) 54
Triplet Etude 54
The Chords in the Key of F 55
Accompaniment Styles 55
May 55
March Majestic 56
Sixteenth-Notes 57
Table of Notes and Rests 57
Sixteenth-Notes 57
Prelude 58
Single String Sixteenths 58
The Notes on the Second String 59
The C Scale in Thirds 59
Notes on the Fifth Fret 59
The Key of D Minor (Relative to F Major) 60
The D Minor Scales 60
The Chords in the Key of D Minor 60
Accompaniment Styles (Common Time) 60
Prelude in D Minor 61
Mist in the Valley 62
The Key of D Major 63
The D Major Scale 63
The Chords in the Key of D Major 63
Accompaniment Styles 63
The D Scale in Two Octaves 64
The Street of Laredo 64
Smoky Mountain Lullaby 65
Thirds in the Key of D 66
Drink to Me Only With Thine Eyes 66
The Key of B Minor (Relative to D Major) 67
The B Minor Scales 67
Etude in B Minor 67
The Chords in the Key of B Minor 68
Accompaniment Styles 68
Southern Picking 68
Love Song 69
Etude 70
The Key of A 71
Etude 71
The Chords in the Key of A 71
The Musical Notation of the Chords 71
Accompaniment Styles 72
Six-Eight Time 72
The Carnival of Venice 72
The Notes on the Third String 73
The G Scale 73
The A Scale 73
G String Etude 73
The Notes of the Fourth String 74
A Table of Notes on the First, Second, Third and Fourth Strings 74
Smooth 74
Tenting Tonight 75
The Key of F♯ Minor (Relative to A Major) 77
Two F♯ Minor Scales 77
The Chords in the Key of F♯ Minor 77
Accompaniment Styles 77
The Key of E Major 78
The Chords in the Key of E Major 78
Careless Love 79
More Chromatic Signs 80
Ode to Bob 80
Chopin's Prelude 82
Spanish Fandango 83
Just As I Am 86
John Henry 88
Me and Merle 90
Wimoweh 93
Liebestraum 97
Czardas 100
Yankee Doodle Dixie 104

Mel Bay

Chet Atkins needs no introduction.

Very few men have created a style of guitar playing that has the public appeal and following that Chet has.

Success and world wide recognition is richly deserved to this man who is not only a great artist but is also a wonderful person.

This is not a method but an elementary approach to the Chet Atkins style of guitar playing. The basic fundamental rudiments are presented in order to elevate the player into this style with ease.

We feel that for the first time a carefully graded approach to the Chet Atkins style is being presented in this publication.

Take your time and enjoy each page as no effort has been spared in making it a real musical treat for you.

Mel Bay

Tuning the Guitar

The six open strings of the guitar will be of the same pitch as the six notes shown in the illustration of the piano keyboard. Note that five of the strings are below the middle C of the piano keyboard.

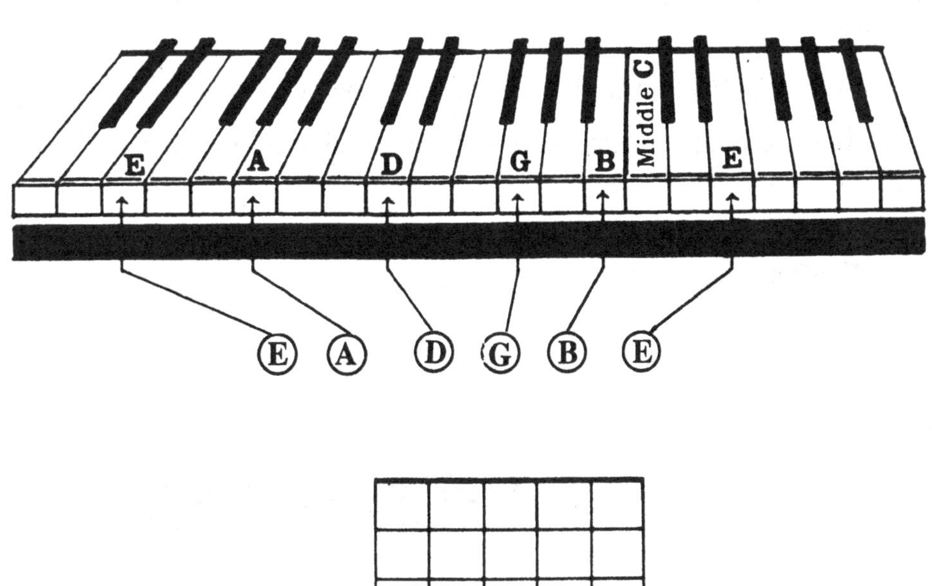

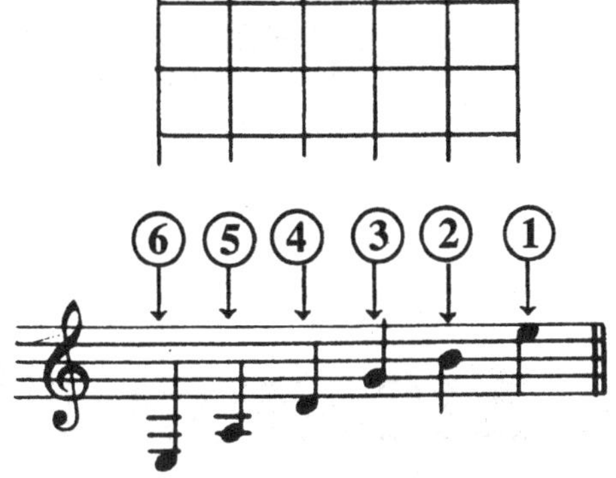

PIANO NOTATION

GUITAR NOTATION

Strings

6th 5th 4th 3rd 2nd 1st

E A D G B E

Another Method of Tuning

1. Tune the 6th string in unison to the E or twelfth white key to the **left of middle** C on the piano.

2. Place the finger behind the fifth fret of the 6th string. This will give you the tone or pitch of the 5th string. (A)

3. Place finger behind the fifth fret of the 5th string to get the pitch of the 4th string. (D)

4. Repeat same procedure to obtain the pitch of the 3rd string. (G)

5. Place finger behind the **fourth fret** of the 3rd string to get the pitch of the 2nd string. (B)

6. Place finger behind the fifth fret of the 2nd string to get the pitch of the 1st string. (E)

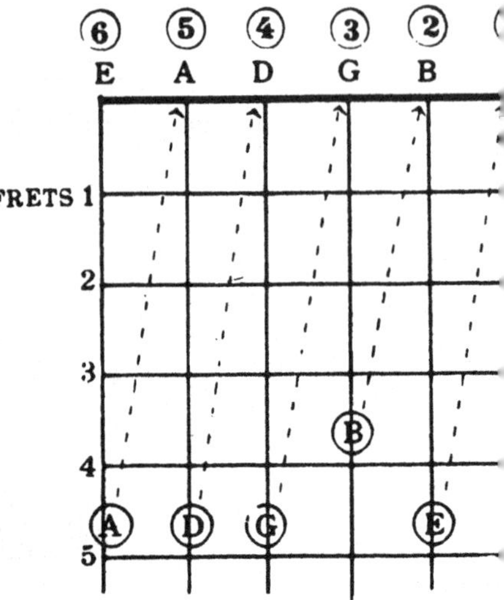

Pitch Pipes

Pitch pipes with instructions for their usage may be obtained at any music store. Each pipe will have the correct pitch of each guitar string and are recommended to be used when a piano is not available.

Electronic Tuners

Various types of electronic tuners are also available.

The Rudiments of Music

The Staff

Music is written on a **Staff** consisting of **five lines** and **four spaces**.

The lines and spaces are numbered upward as shown:

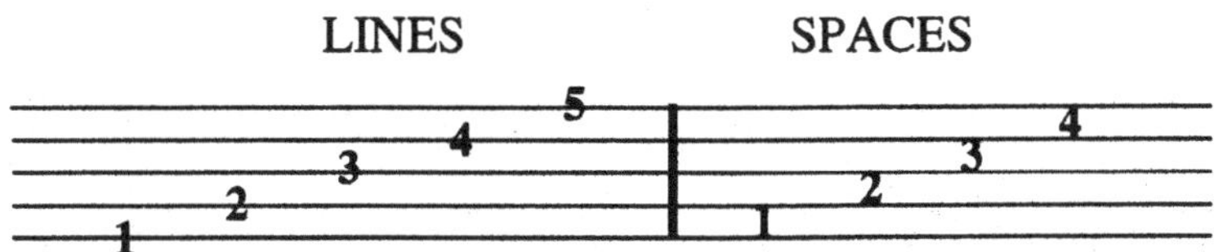

They also have **Letter** names.

The **Lines** are named as follows: 1-E, 2-G, 3-B, 4-D, 5-F.

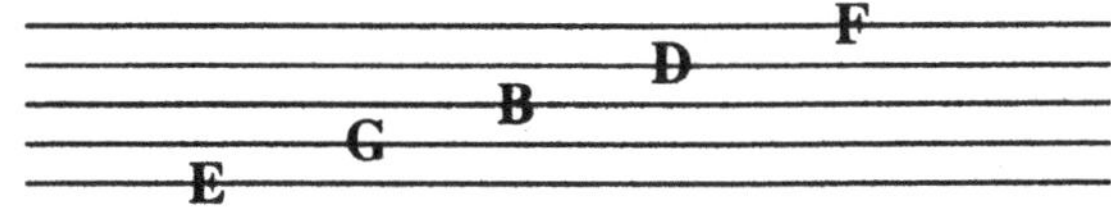

The letters can easily be remembered by the sentence:

Every **G**ood **B**oy **D**oes **F**ine

The letter-names of the **Spaces** are 1-F, 2-A, 3-C, 4-E

They spell the word **F-A-C-E**.

The musical alphabet has seven letter—A, B, C, D, E, F, G.

The Clef

This sign 𝄞 is the **Treble** or **G Clef**.

All guitar music will be written in this clef.

The **staff** is divided into **measures** by vertical lines called **bars**.

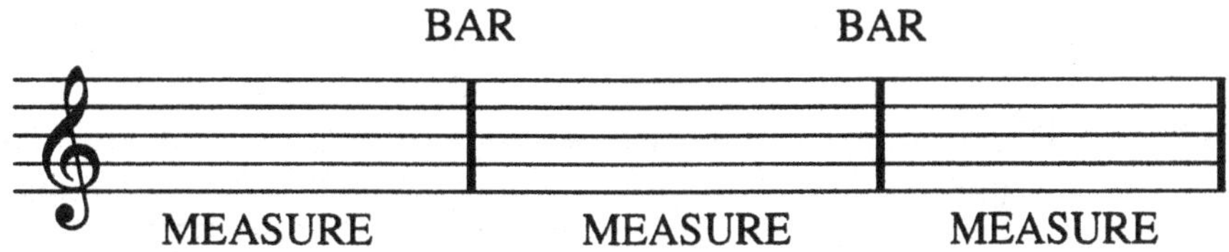

Double bars mark the end of a section or strain of music.

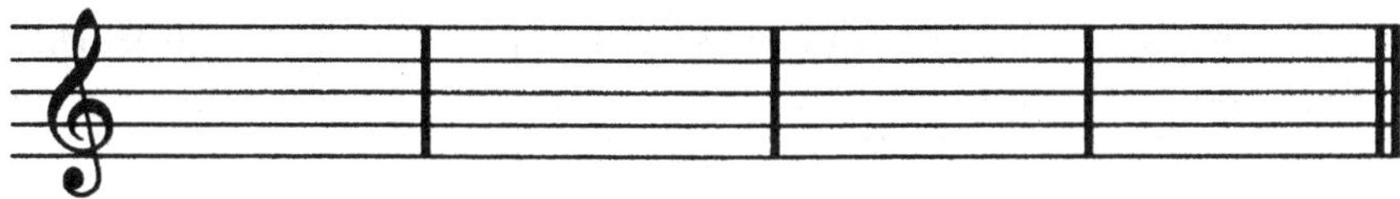

Notes

This is a **Note**:

A note has three parts.

They are — the **Head** , the **Stem** , and the **Flag** .

Notes may be placed in the staff,

above the staff,

and

below the staff.

A note will bear the name of the line or space it occupies on the staff.

The location of a note in, above, or below the staff will indicate the Pitch.

Pitch: the highness or lowness of a tone.

Tone: a musical sound.

This is a **Whole Note.** The head is hollow. It does not have a stem.

This is a **Half Note**. The head is hollow. It has a stem.

This is a **Quarter Note**. The head is solid. It has a stem.

This is an **Eighth Note**. The head is solid. It has a stem and a flag.

Note Values

= 4 Beats

A **Whole-Note** will receive four beats or counts.

= 2 Beats

A **Half-Note** will receive two beats or counts.

= 1 Beat

A **Quarter Note** will receive one beat or count.

= 1/2 Beat

An **Eighth-Note** will receive one-half beat or count. (2 for 1 beat)

Rests

A **Rest** is a sign used to designate a period of silence.

This period of silence will be of the same duration of time as the note to which it corresponds.

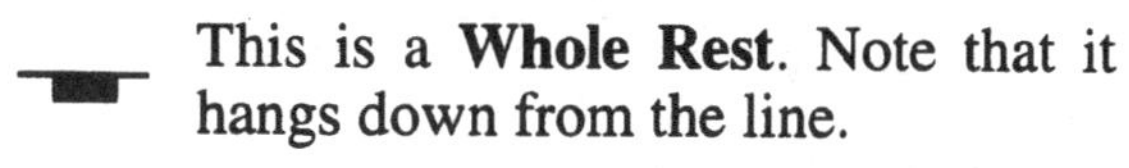
This is a **Whole Rest**. Note that it hangs down from the line.

This is a **Half Rest.** Note that it lays on the line.

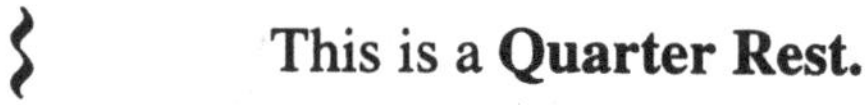
This is a **Quarter Rest.**

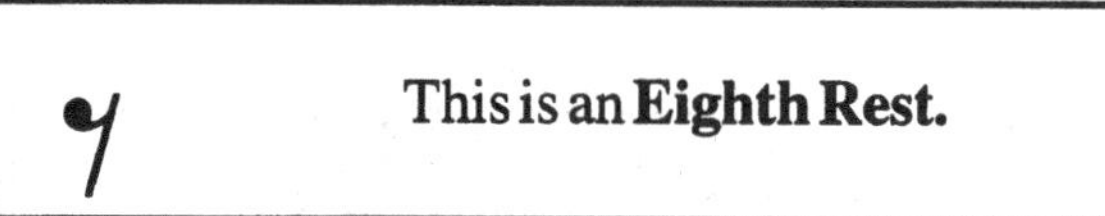
This is an **Eighth Rest.**

Notes and Comparative Rests

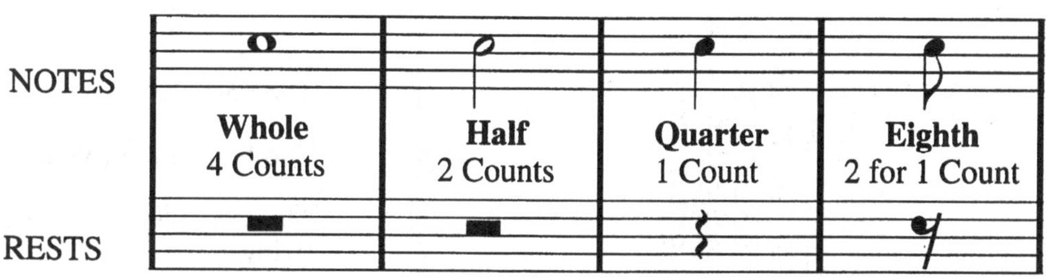

The Time Signature

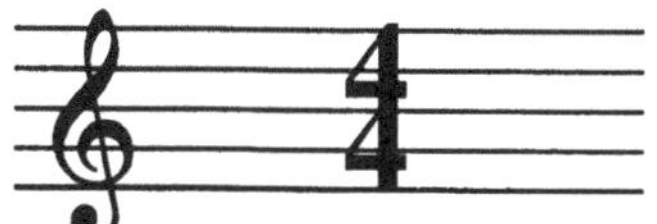

The above examples are the common types of time signatures to be used in this book.

4 The **Top Number** indicates the *number of beats per measure.*

4 The **Bottom Number** indicates the *type of note receiving one beat.*

4/4 time and **Common-Time** are the same.

4—beats per measure.

4—a quarter-note receives one beat.

4/4 (or Common) Time

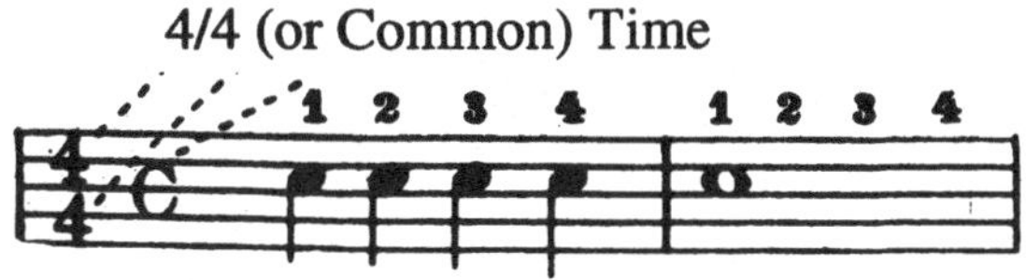

How to Count 4/4 Time

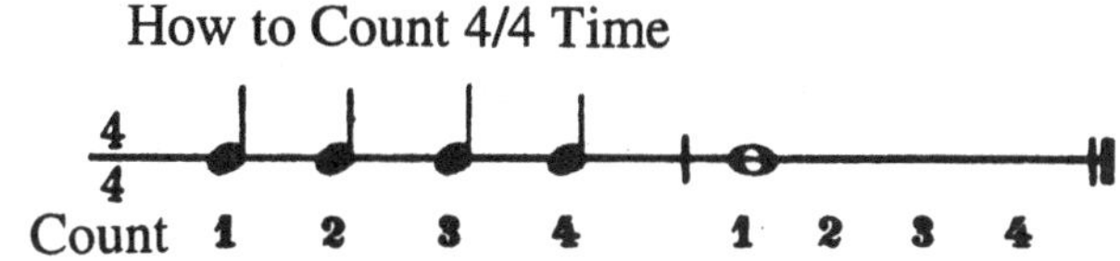

Ledger Lines

When the pitch of a musical sound is below or above the staff, the notes are then placed on, or between, extra lines called **ledger lines**.

They will be like this

The Fingerboard

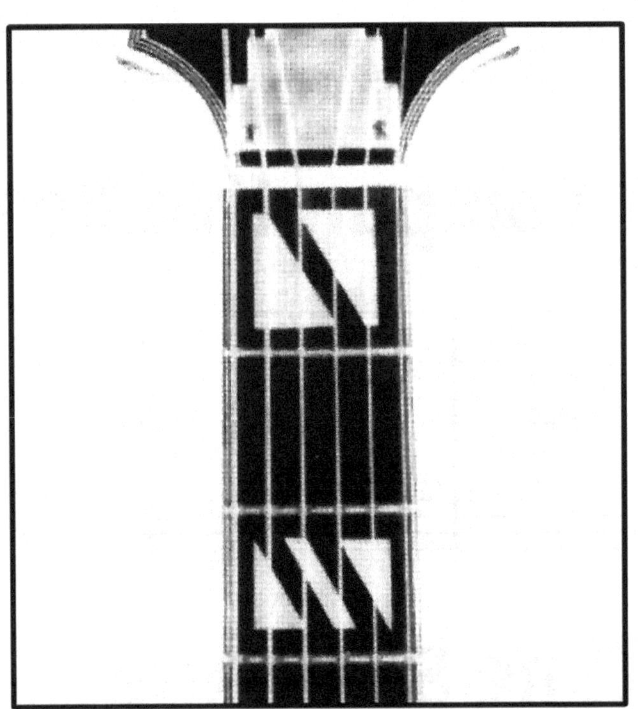

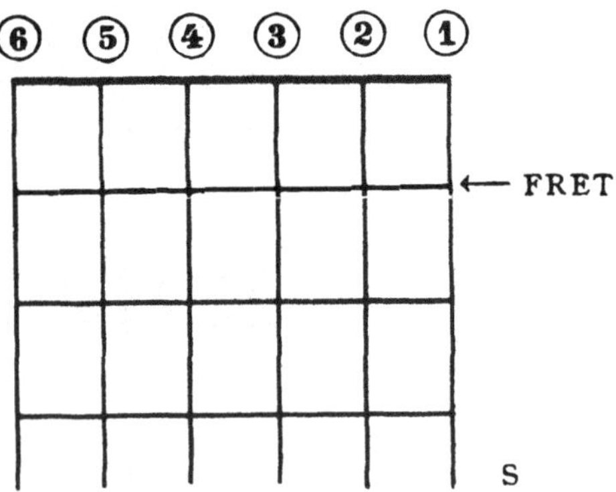

The vertical lines are the strings.

The horizontal lines are the frets.

The encircled numbers are the number of the strings.

String-Numbers: The encircled numbers 6 5 4 3 2 1 will be the numbers of the strings.

Charts

The charts used in this book will have the **vertical-lines** as the **strings** and the **horizontal-lines** as the **frets.**

Reading from left to right the strings will be ⑥⑤④③②①.

The Correct Way To Hold the Guitar

The Right Hand (R.H.)

The right hand fingers will be designated as:

p = Thumb

i = First or Index Finger

m =Second or Middle Finger

a =Third or Ring Finger

t =Left hand thumb

Tablature

(Diagrams)

The Fingerboard

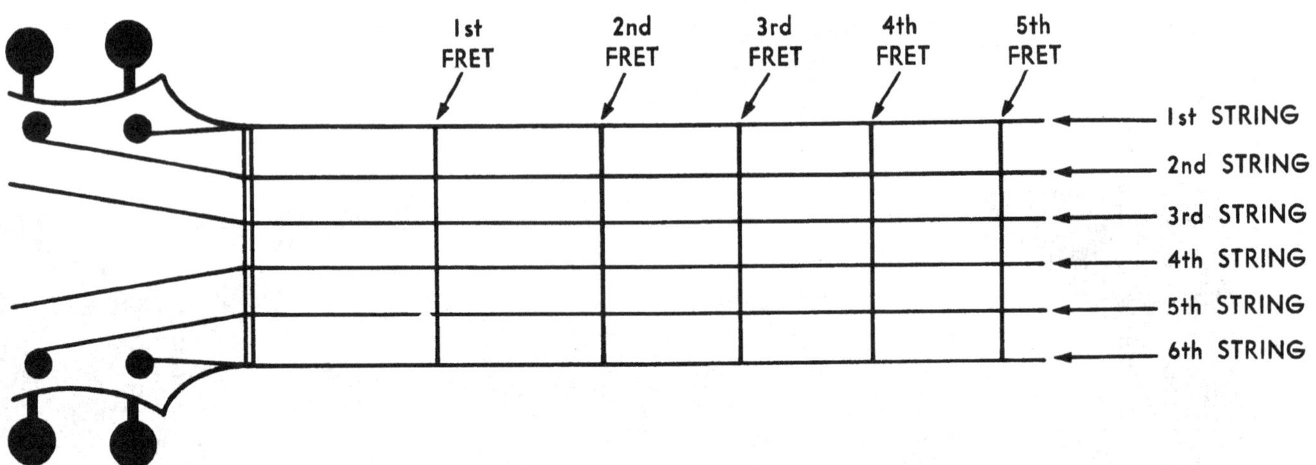

Tablature (Diagram)

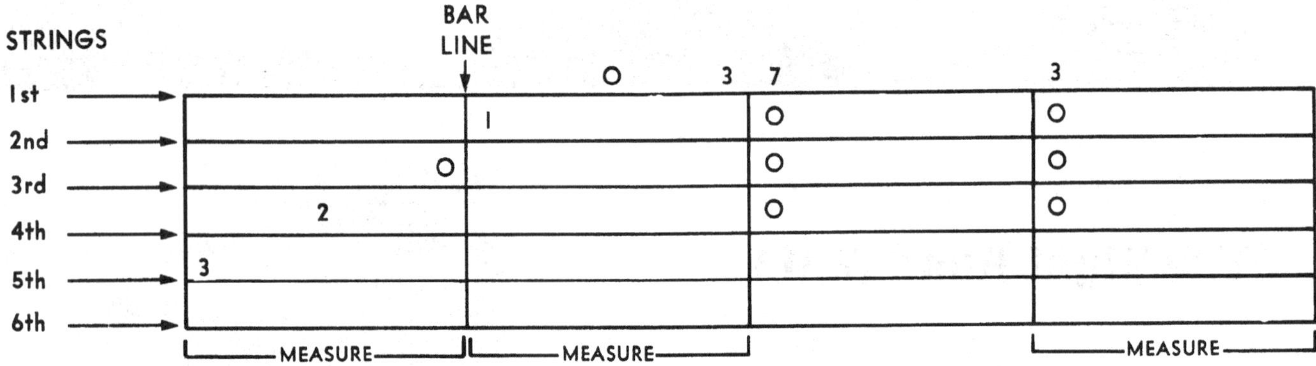

The lines represent the strings of the guitar.

The numbers represent the frets. O indicates open string.

When a number is above the top line it will be played on the first string. When a number is above the second line from the top, it will be played on the second string, etc.

In the example above, the number 3 in the first measure indicates the 3rd fret on the fifth string.

The number 2 indicates the 2nd fret, fourth string. The O indicates the third string open.

In the third measure the number 7 indicates the 7th fret on the first string. The second, third, and fourth strings are open. The four strings will be stuck simultaneously as a chord.

The Notes on the Sixth String (E)

All notes shown in this book will be in the FIRST POSITION.
The FIRST POSITION ranges from the first to the fourth frets.
OUR FIRST STUDY: Three notes on the 6th string.

They are:

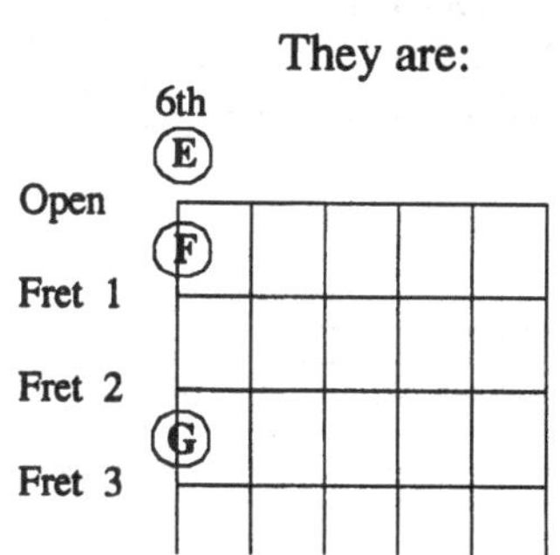

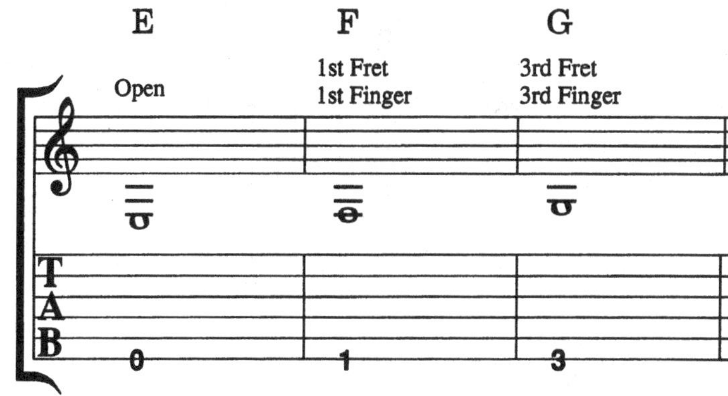

Note that the number of the fret and finger is identical.

Employ the right hand thumb only in playing the following pieces. (P)
WHOLE-NOTES: A WHOLE-NOTE (o) receives FOUR BEATS.
It is struck on the first beat and held for the remaining three.

(Count) 1 - 2 - 3 - 4

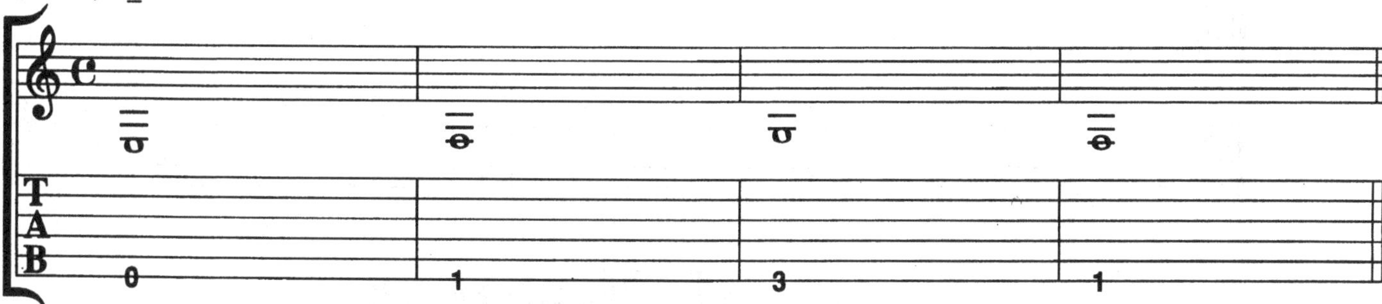

HALF-NOTES: A HALF-NOTE (𝅗𝅥) receives TWO BEATS.

(Count) 1 - 2 - 3 - 4

QUARTER-NOTES: A QUARTER-NOTE (♩) receives ONE BEAT.

(Count) 1 - 2 - 3 - 4

The Notes on the Fifth String (A)

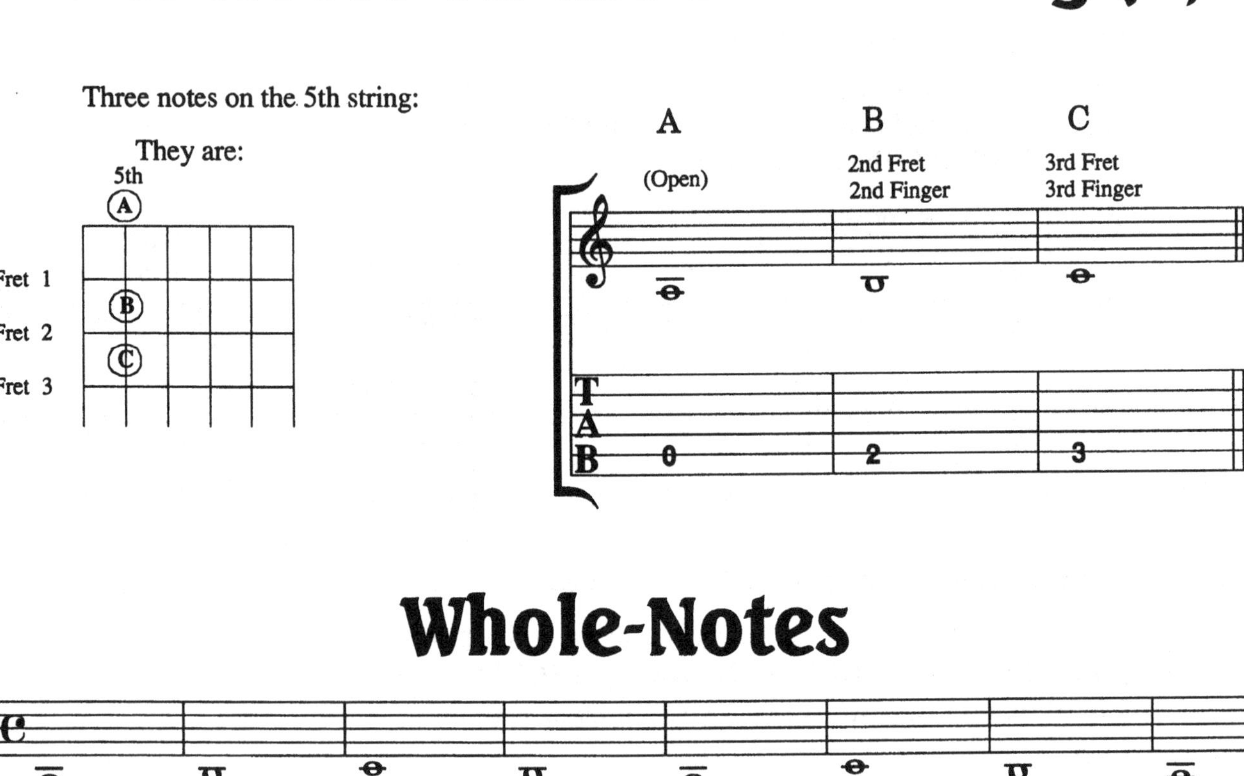

Whole-Notes

Half-Notes

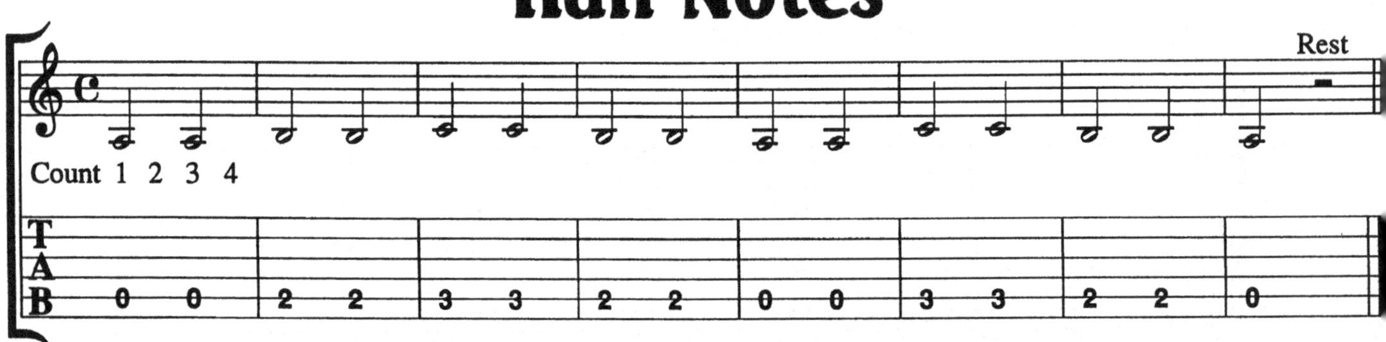

Quarter-Notes

The Notes on the Fourth String (D)

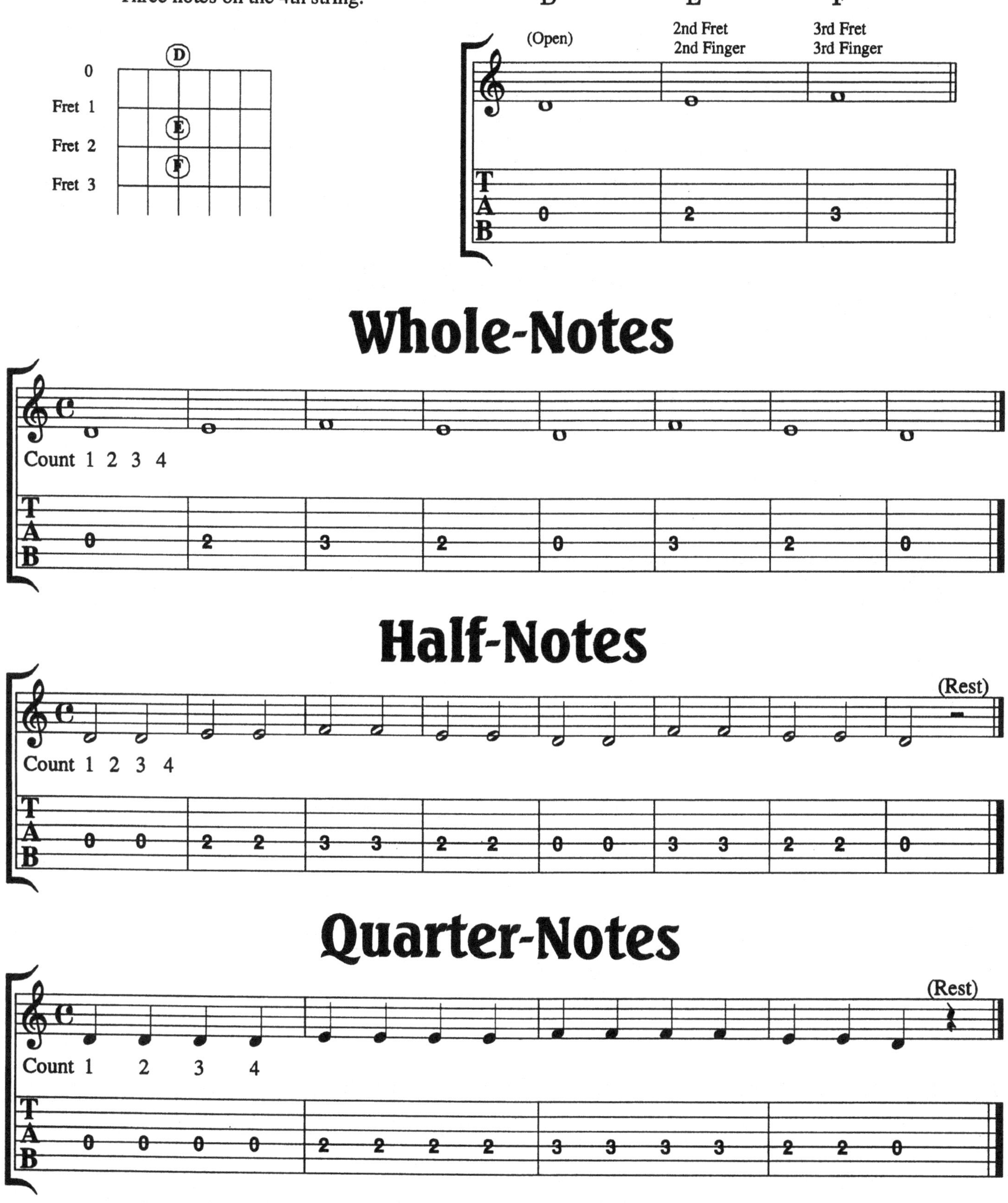

Unless otherwise shown, all notes on the 6, 5 & 4 strings will be plucked with the right hand thumb.

The Notes on the E⑥, A⑤, and D④ Strings

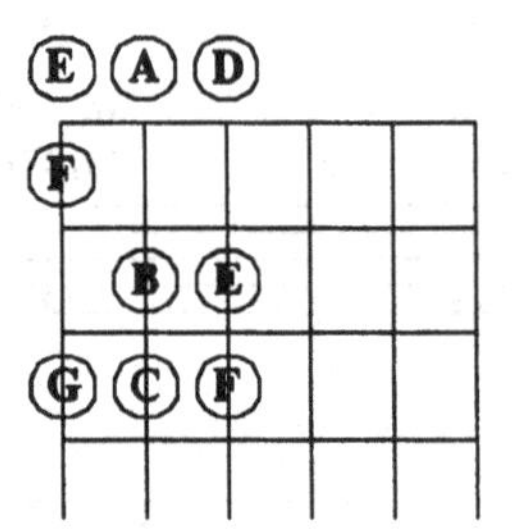

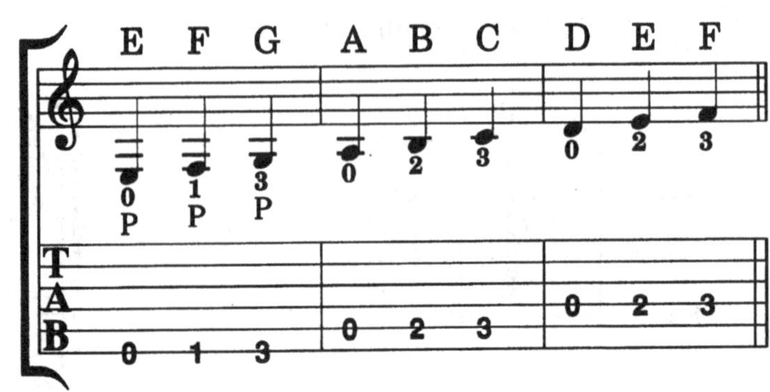

The Six Five Jive

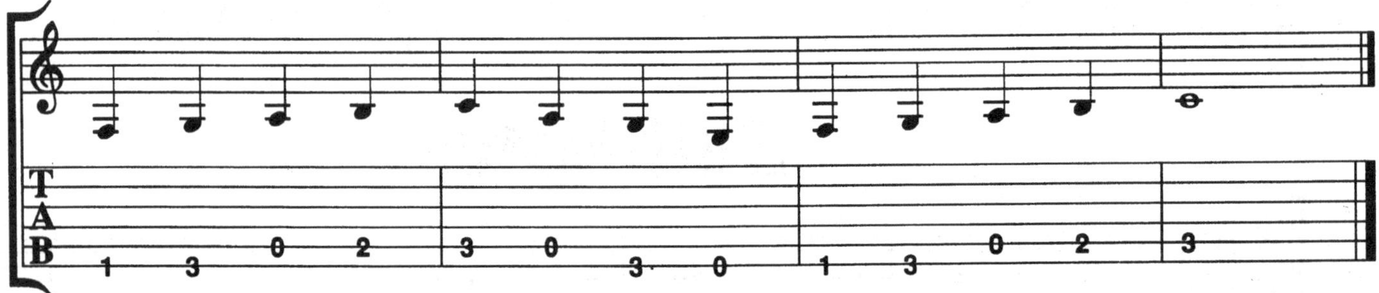

Yankee Doodle

How Can I Leave Thee

The Notes on the Third String (G)

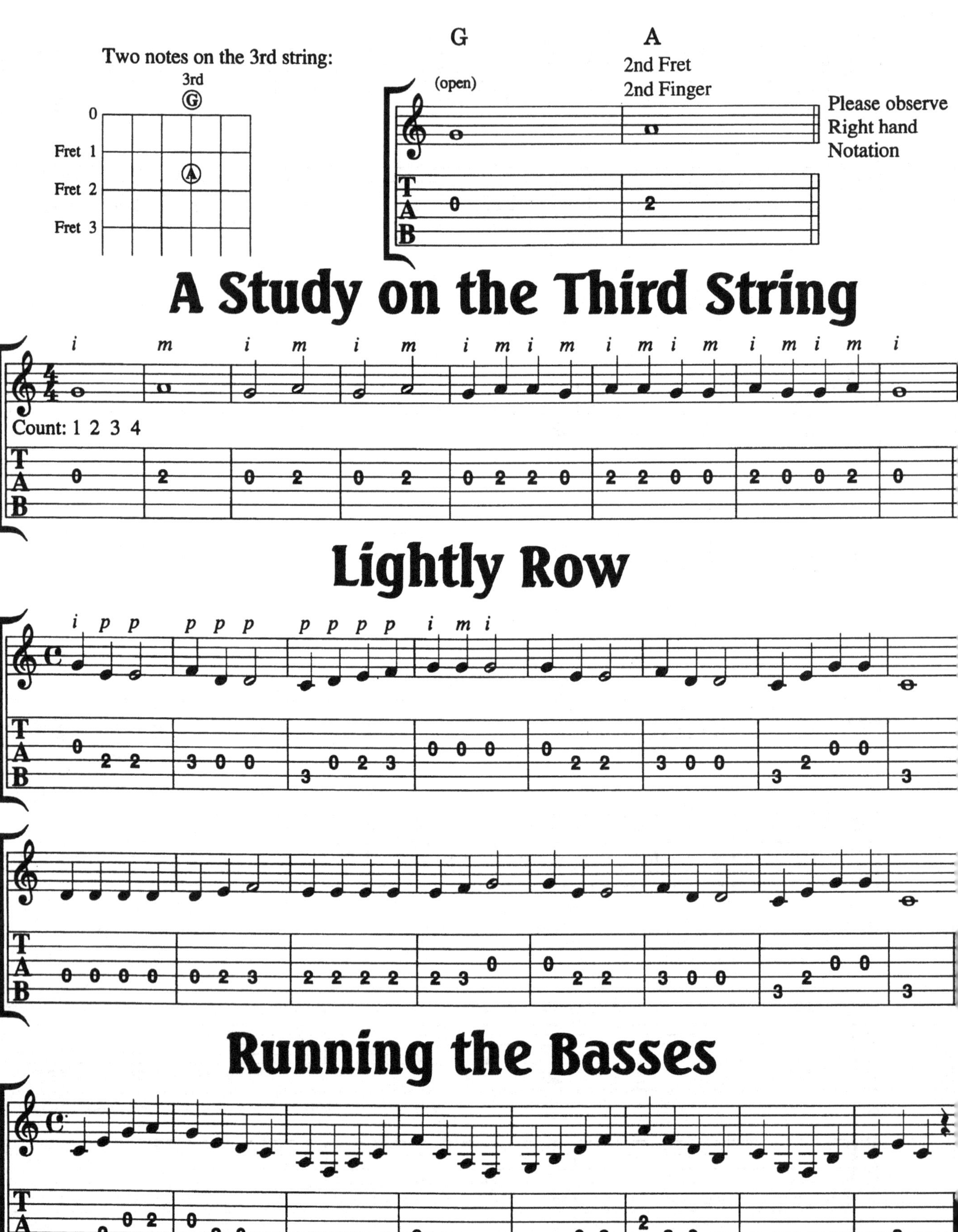

The Notes on the Second String (B)

Three notes on the 2nd string:

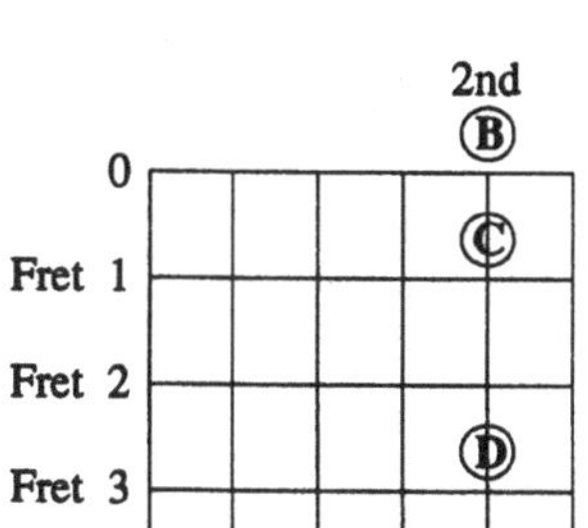

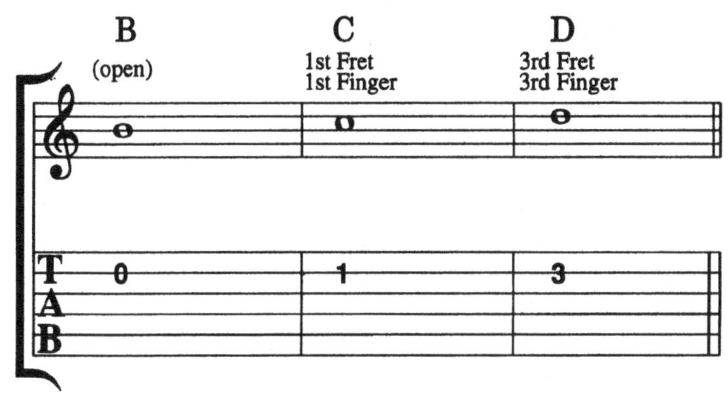

Whole-Notes

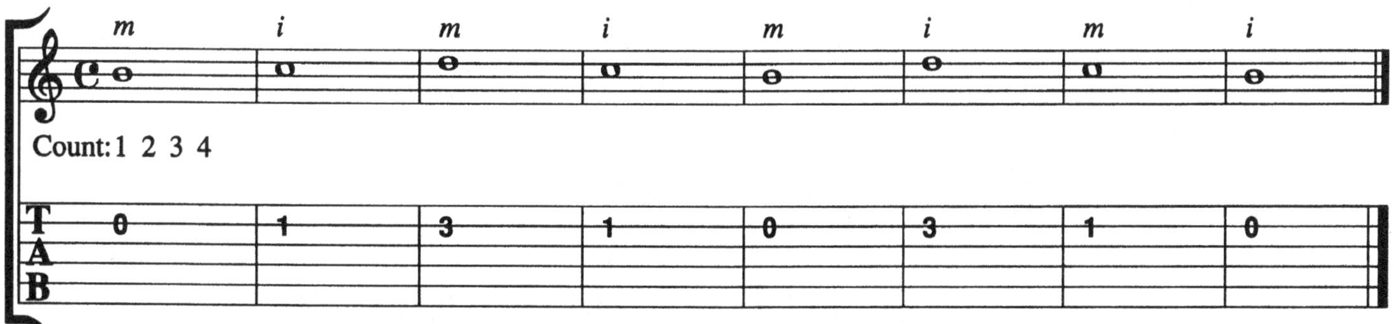

Half-Notes

Quarter-Notes

The Notes on the First String (E)

Four notes on the 1st string:

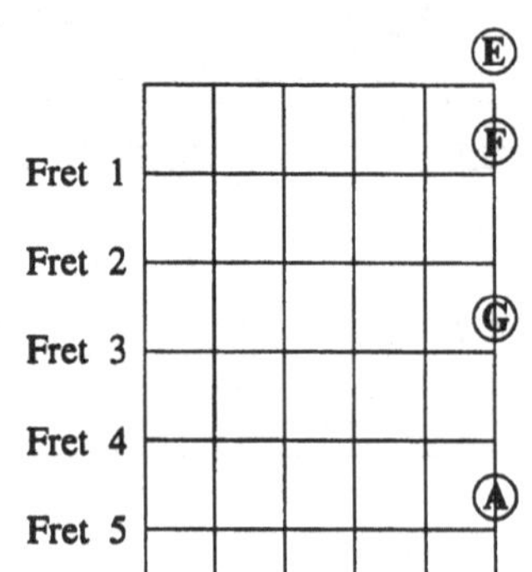

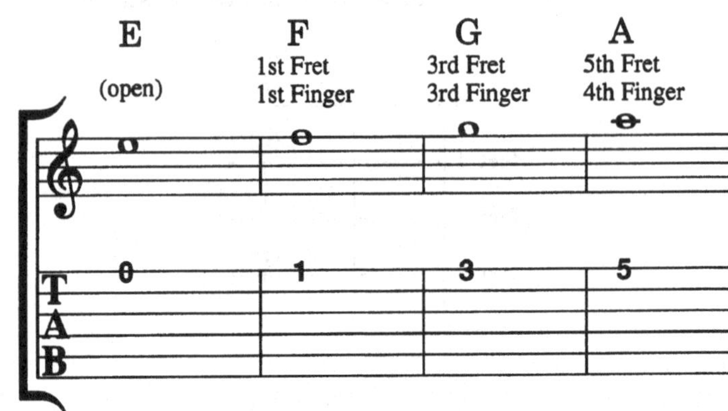

Three-Four Time

This sign  indicates three-four time.

3 - - beats per measure.
4 - - type of note receiving one beat. (quarter - note)

In three-four time, we will have three beats per measure.
A quarter note will receive one beat.

Dotted Half-Notes

A dot (·) placed behind a note increases its value by one-half.
A dotted half-note (𝅗𝅥.) will receive three beats.

Colonial Waltz

Right Hand Development
Alpha

Dots before and after a double bar mean repeat the measures between.

Two String Harmony

When two or more notes are on the same stem play them simultaneously.

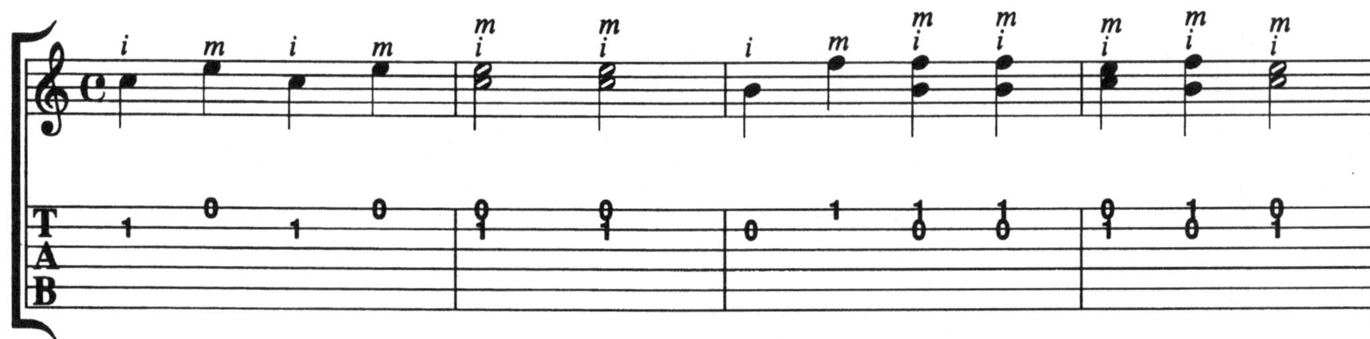

A Picking Study

Pick Up Notes

One or more notes at the beginning of a strain before the first measure are referred to as pick up notes. The pick up notes are taken from the last measure of the selections. Note that the last measure has only three beats.

Two and One

* The first finger should lay flat on the first and second string.

** use the fourth finger on D note.

Repeat the above Study until mastered.

Tone

Music is composed of sounds pleasant to the ear.
SOUND may be made from NOISE or TONE.
NOISE is made by *irregular vibrations* such as would be caused by striking a table with a hammer, the shot of a gun, or slapping two stones together.
TONE is produced by *regular vibrations* as would be caused by drawing a bow over the strings of a violin, striking the strings of a guitar, or blowing through a wind instrument, such as a trumpet.
A TONE has four charcteristics... PITCH, DURATION, DYNAMICS and TIMBRE.
PITCH: The highness or lowness of a tone.
DURATION: The length of a tone.
DYNAMICS: The force or power of a tone (loudness or softness).
TIMBRE: Quality of the tone.
A NOTE represents the PITCH AND DURATION of a tone.
DYNAMICS are indicated by words such as...

Pianissimo . . . *(pp)* . . . . Very soft
Piano . . . . *(p)* . . . . . . Soft
Mezzo piano . . *(mp)* . . . . Medium soft
Mezzo forte . . *(mf)* . . . . Medium loud
Forte . . . . *(f)* . . . . . Very loud

TIMBRE depends upon the skill of the performer plus the quality of the instrument on which he is playing.

Tempo

Tempo is the *rate of speed* of a musical composition.
Three types of tempo used in this book will be:
ANDANTE: A slow easy pace. MODERATO: Moderate. ALLEGRO: Lively.

The Tie

The TIE is a curved line between two notes of the same pitch.
The first note is played and held for the time duration of both.
The second note is not played but held.

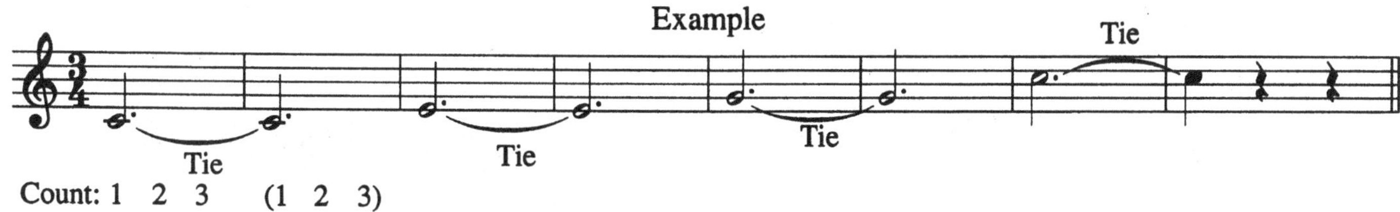

First and Second Endings

Sometimes two endings are required in certain selections.. one to lead back into a repeated chorus and one to close it.

Chromatics

The alteration of the pitches of tones is brought about by the use of symbols called CHROMATICS. (also referred to as ACCIDENTALS)

The Sharp

♯

The SHARP placed before a note raises its pitch $\frac{1}{2}$-step or one fret.

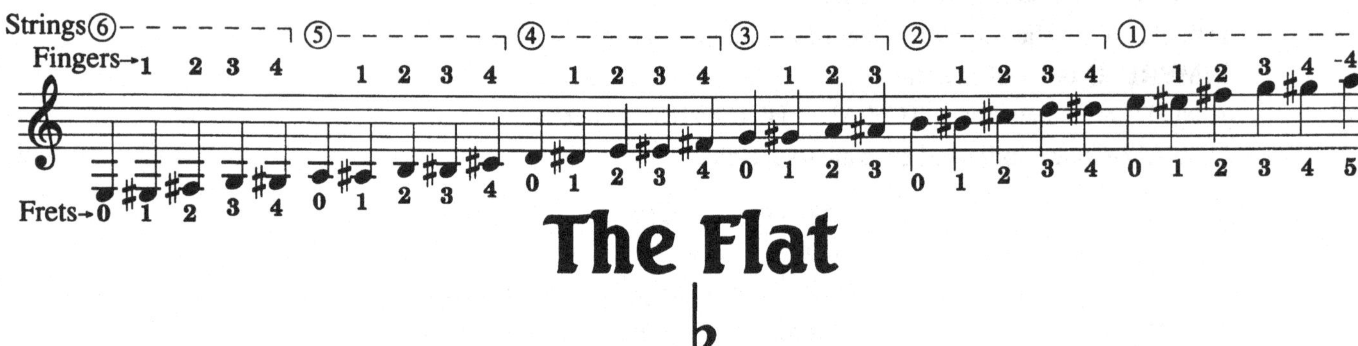

The Flat

♭

The FLAT placed before a note lowers its pitch $\frac{1}{2}$-step or one fret.

The Natural

♮

The NATURAL restores a note to its normal position. It cancels all accidentals previously used. When an accidental appears before a note, that note will be affected through the measure. On leaving the measure, the Accidental will be cancelled.

Accidentally On Purpose

Music in Two Parts

Generally speaking, when music is written in two parts, the notes with the stems turned downward will be plucked with the thumb.

The notes with the stems turned upward will be played with the fingers.

In the example at right the lower note is a dotted half and will be held or sustained for three beats.

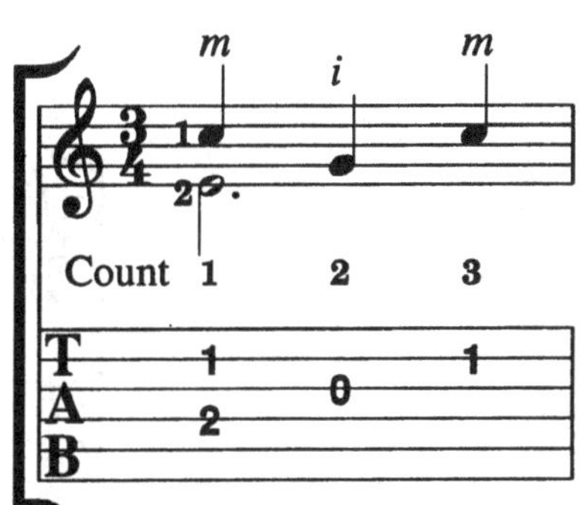

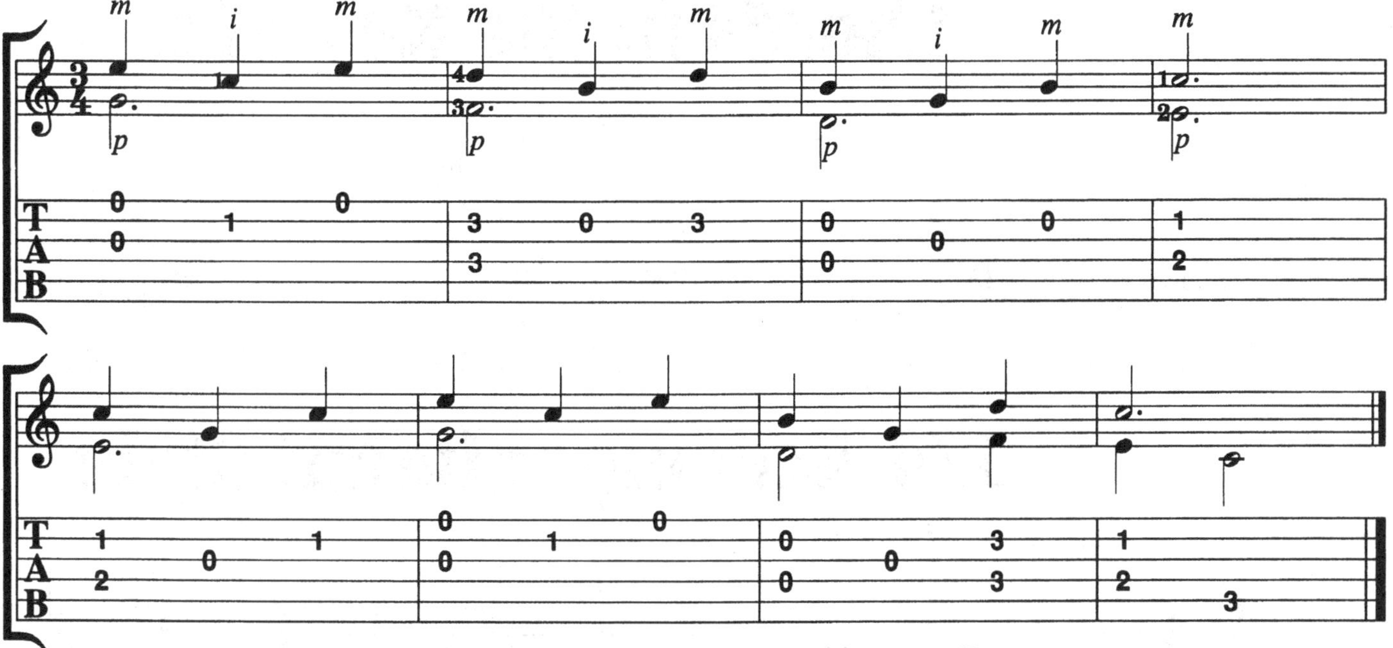

Fingerstyle Etude

The Key of C

The C Scale

Chords in the Key of C

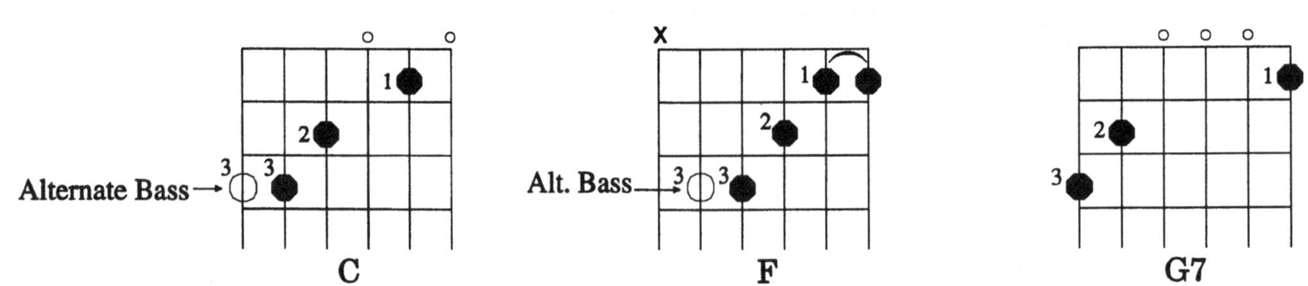

3/4 Accompaniment Style

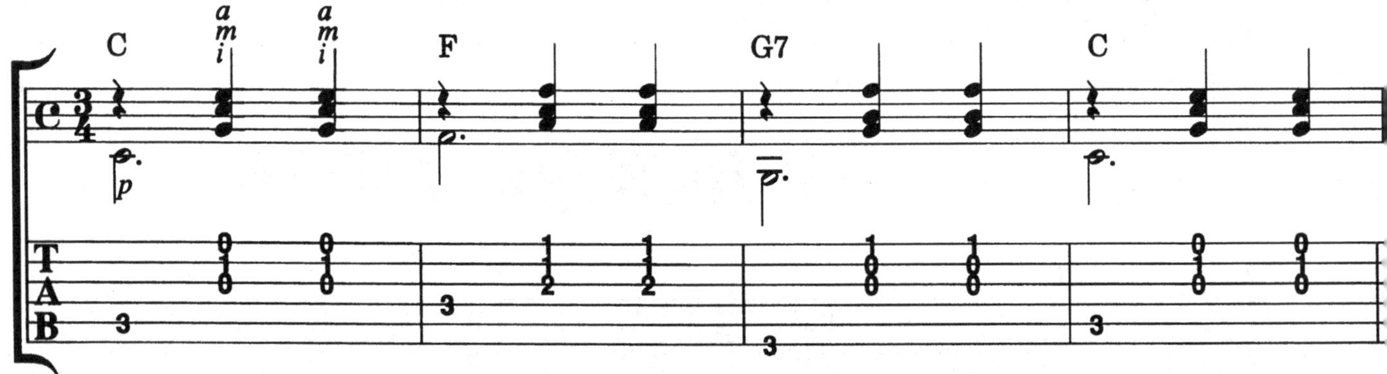

4/4 Accompaniment

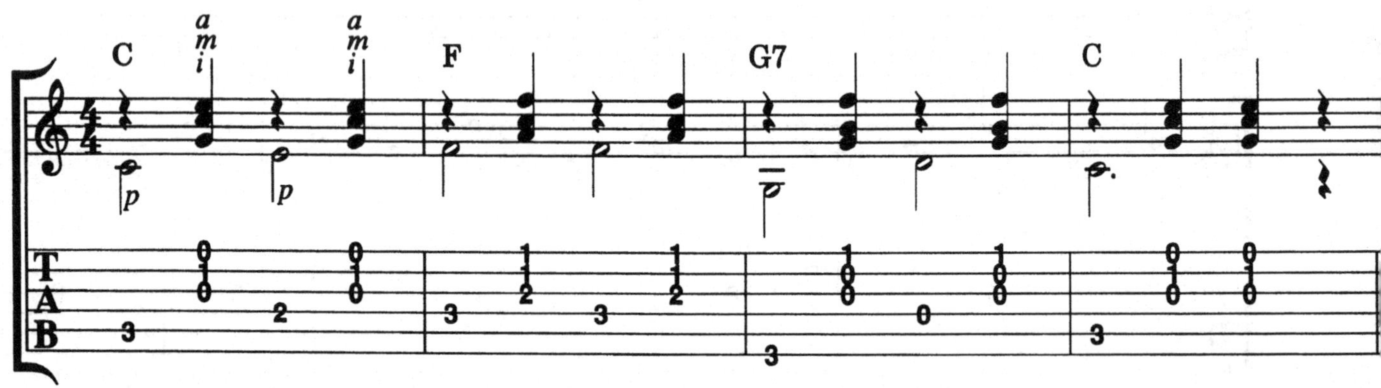

Home, Home, Can I Forget Thee

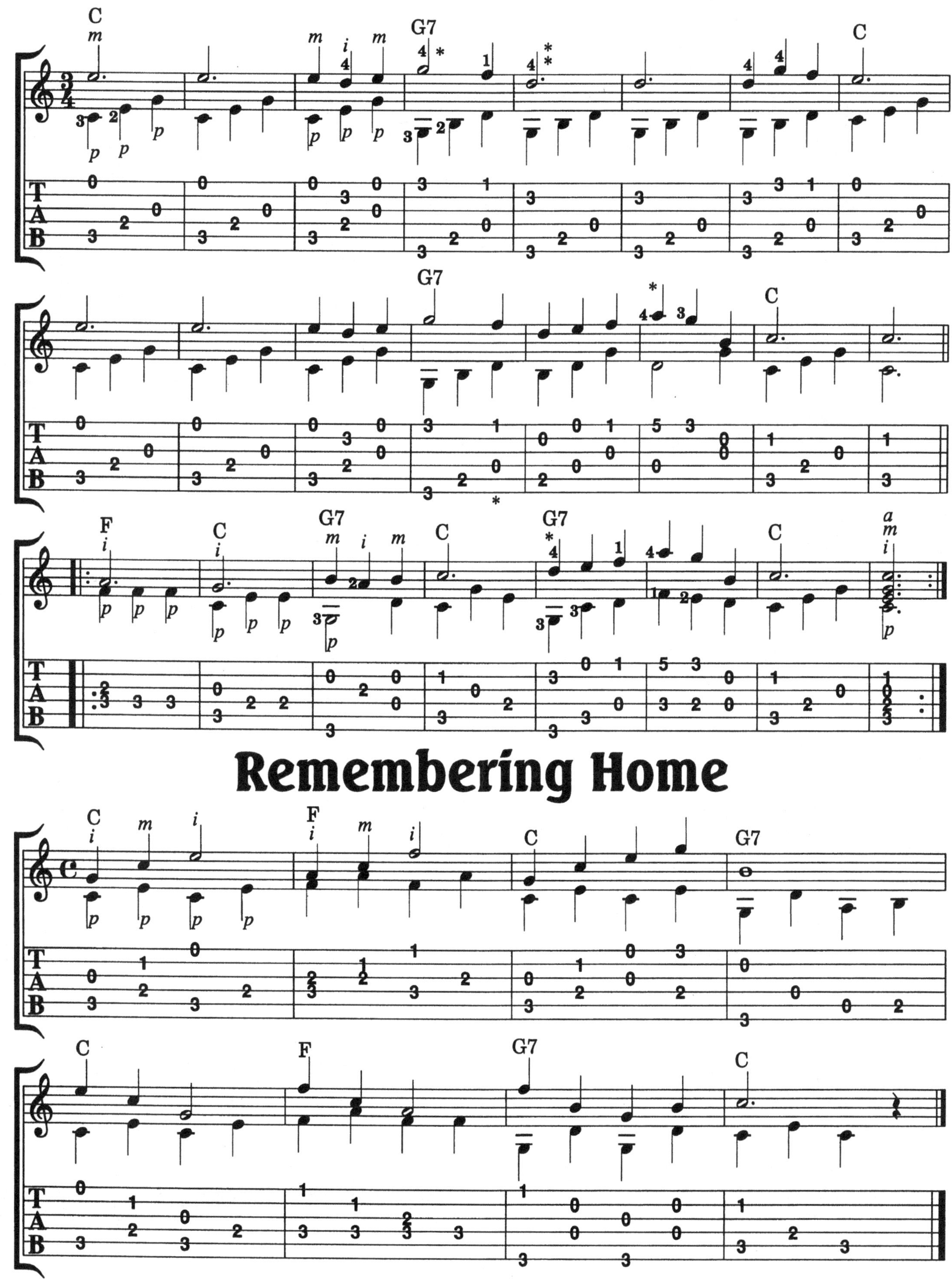

Alternate Basses

Muffle the Bass strings with heel of right hand.
Alternate third finger of left hand from ⑤ to ⑥ string on the third beat, when playing C chord.

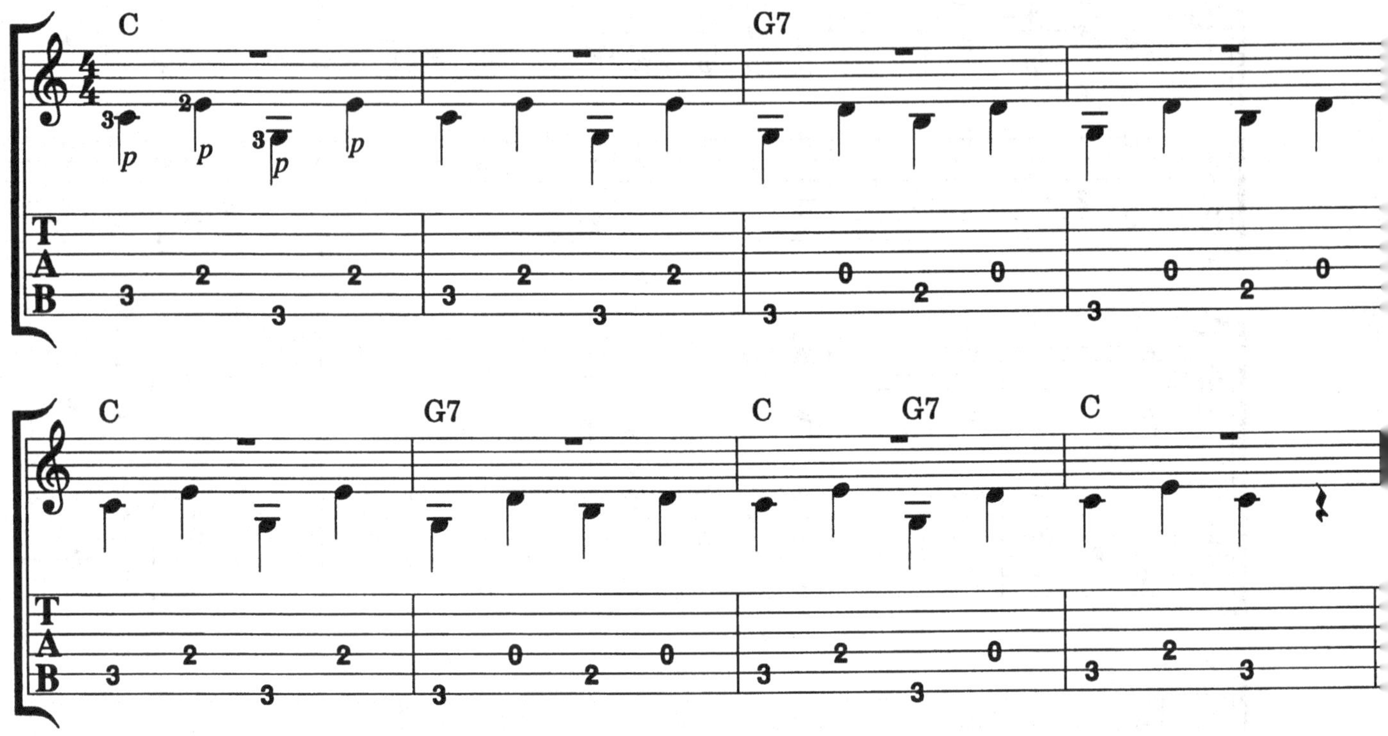

With Melody Notes

Lightly Row

* Use fourth Finger. $\overset{*}{*}$ Do not make full chord use first finger only.

Long, Long Ago

The Marine Hymn

Arr. by Chet Atkins

Martha

Arr. by Chet Atkins

The Eighth Note

An eighth note receives one-half beat. (One quarter note equals two eighth notes). An eighth note will have a head, stem, and flag. If two or more are in successive order they may be connected by a bar. (See Example)

Eighth Notes and Eighth Rests

The Scale in Eighth Notes

A Scale Study

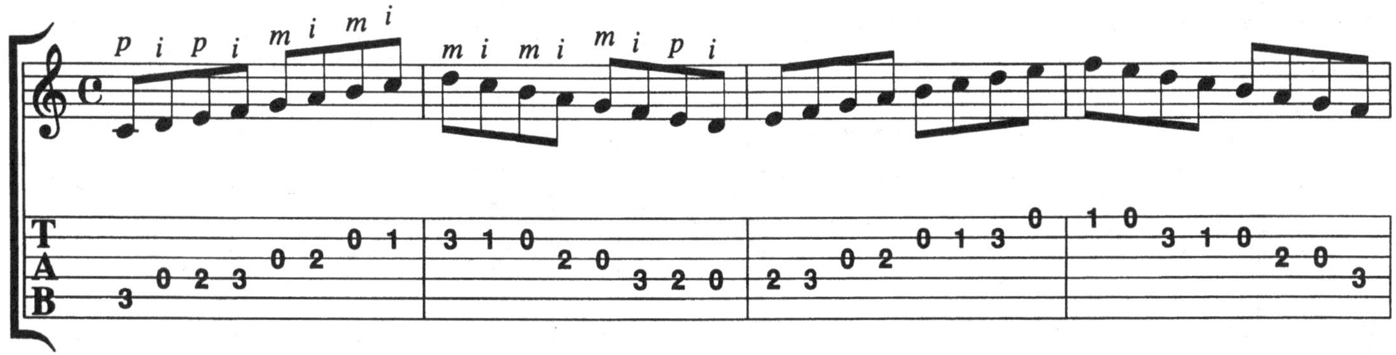

An Eighth Note Study

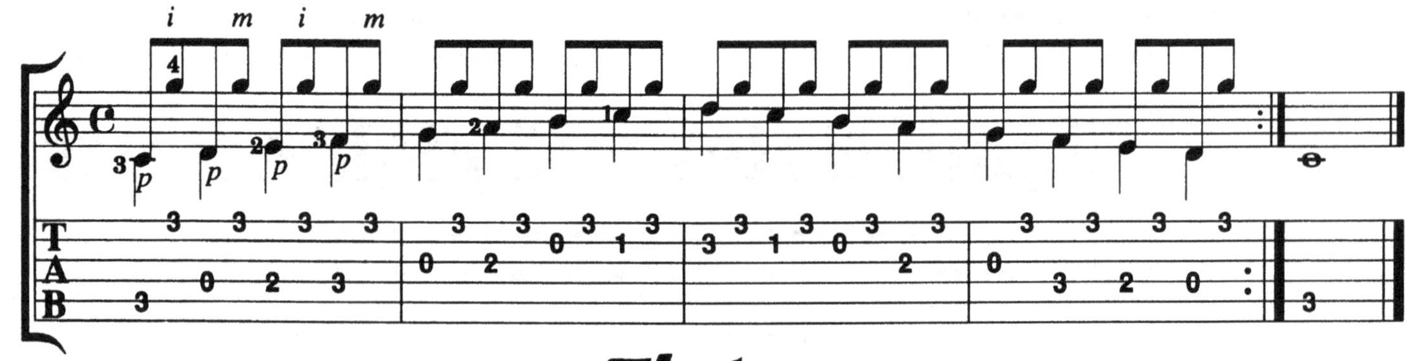

i m i m
p p p p

Tiptoe

C
m i m i m i
F C
1.
D9
G7
Count 1 & 2 & 3 & 4
2.
D9 G C F C D9
G7 C F C D9 G7 C

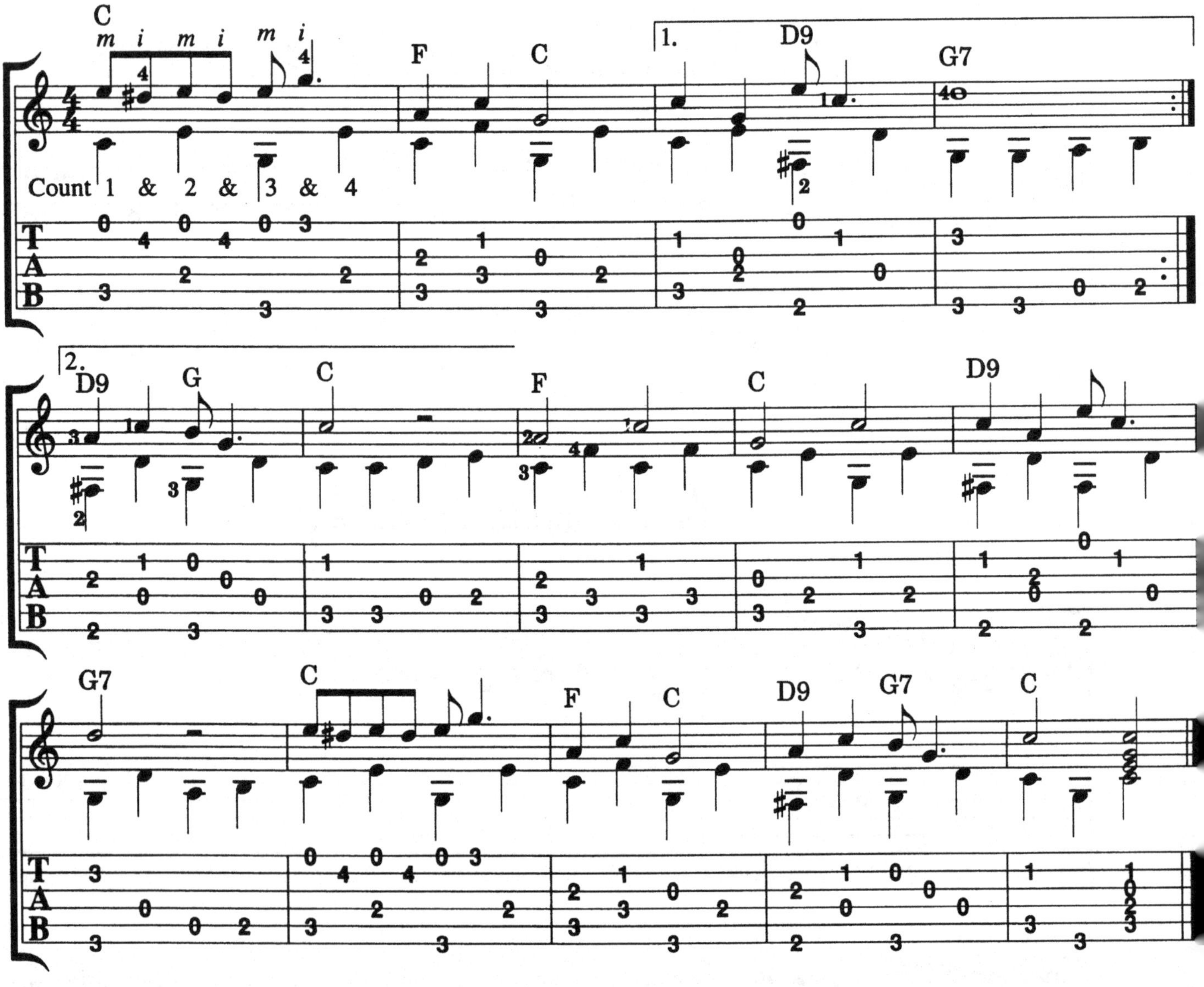

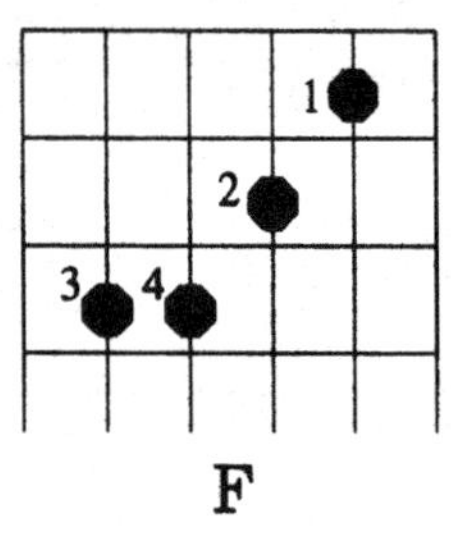

F

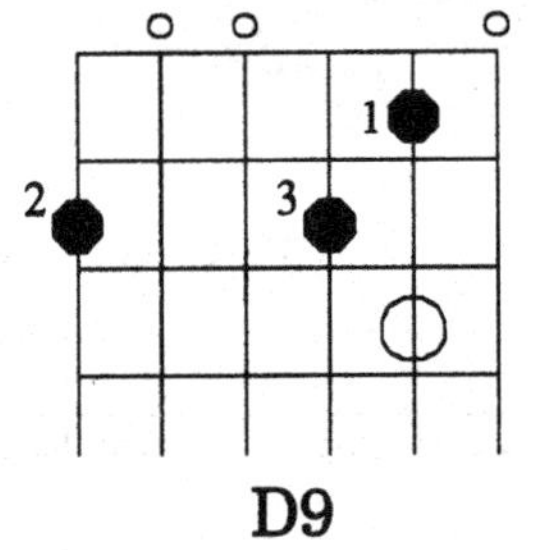

D9

Our Boys Will Shine Tonight

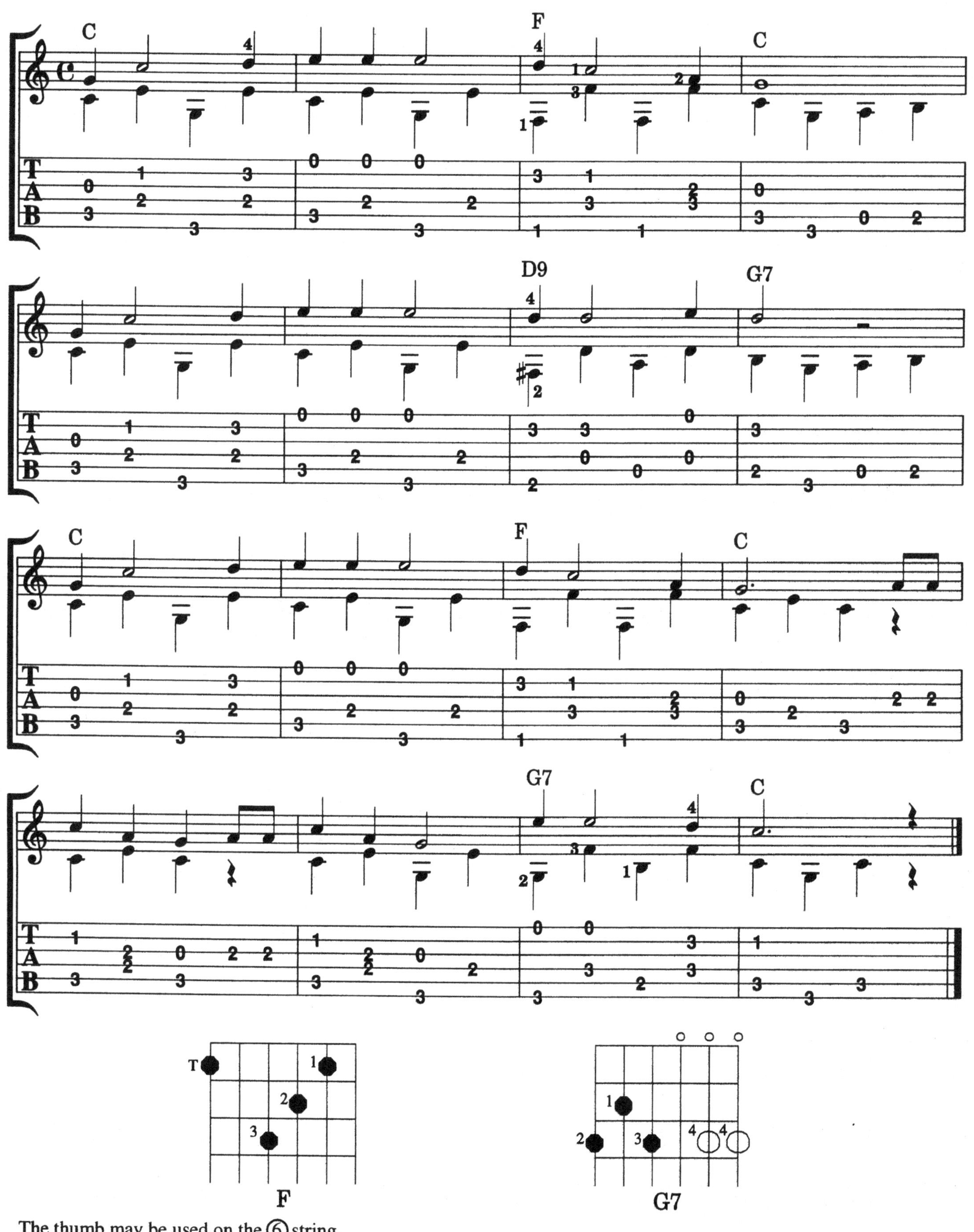

The thumb may be used on the ⑥ string.

The Caissons Go Rolling Along

The Blue Tail Fly

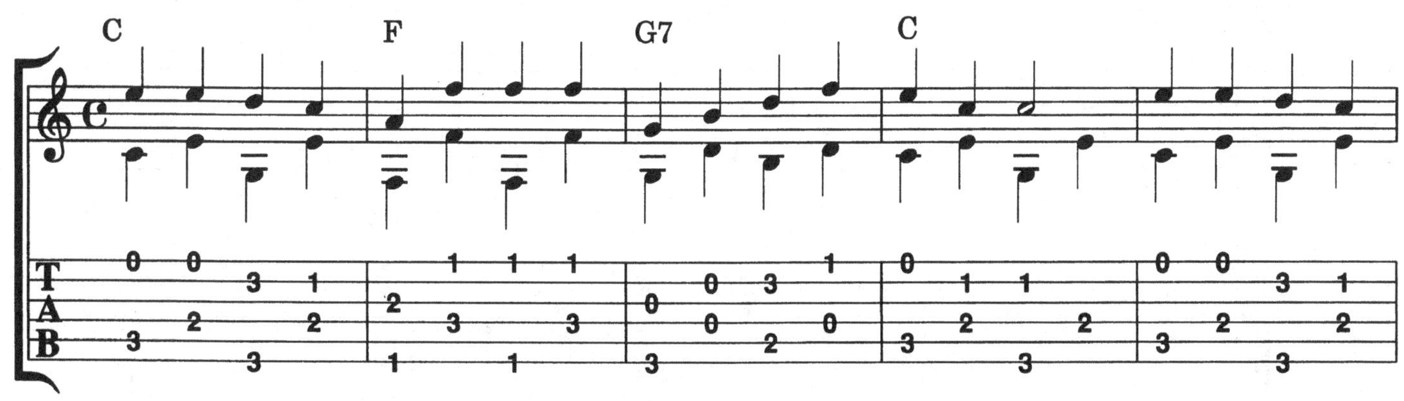

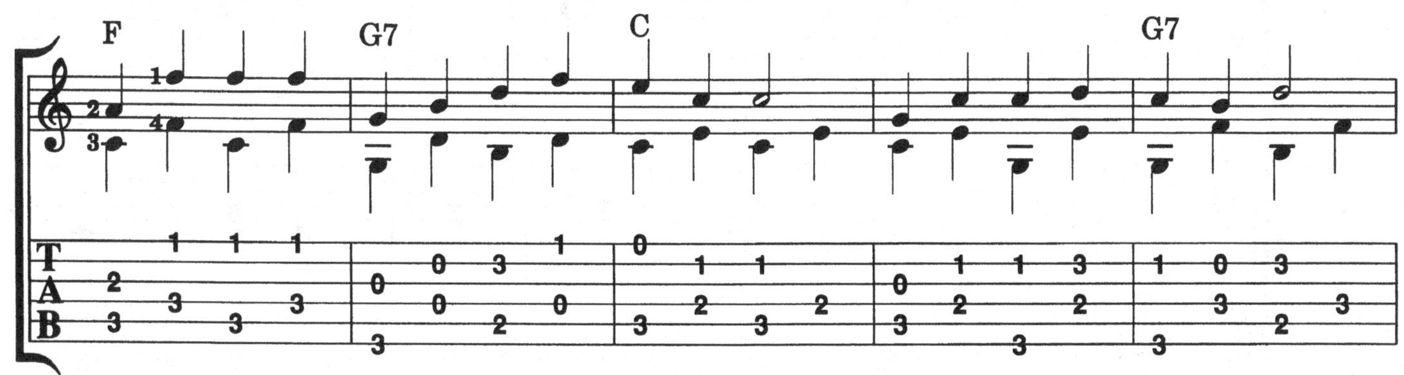

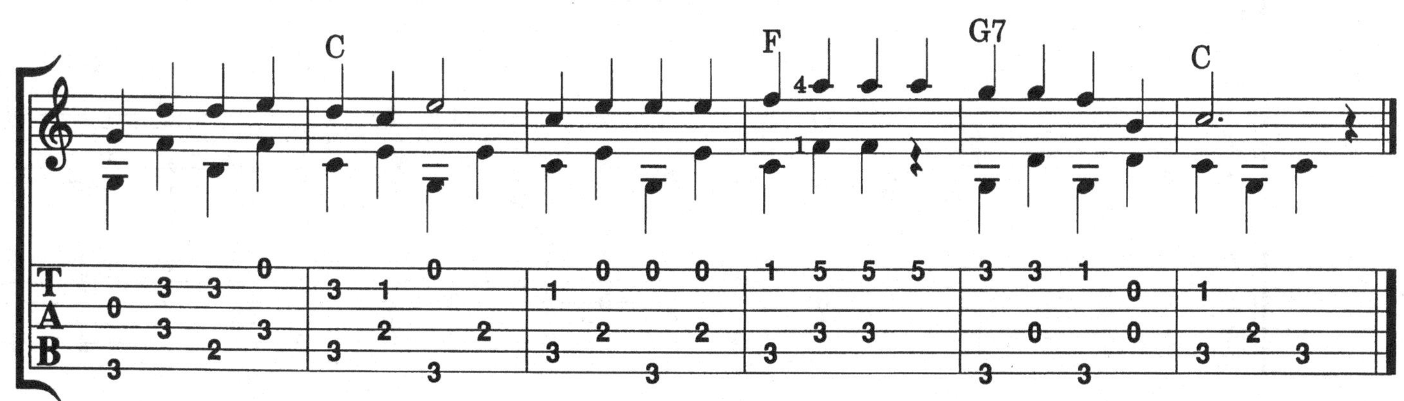

Bicycle Built for Two

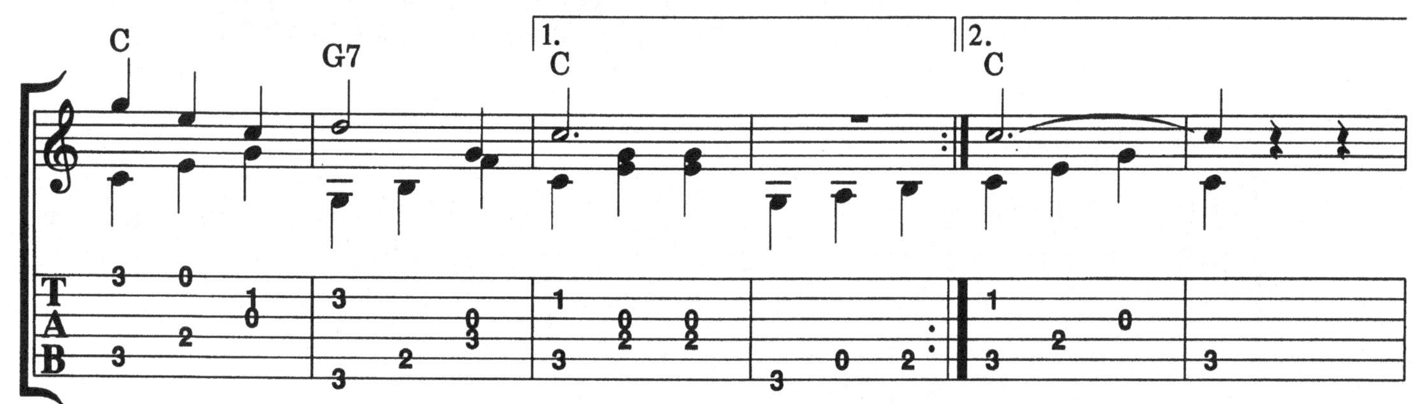

Oh, My Darling Clementine

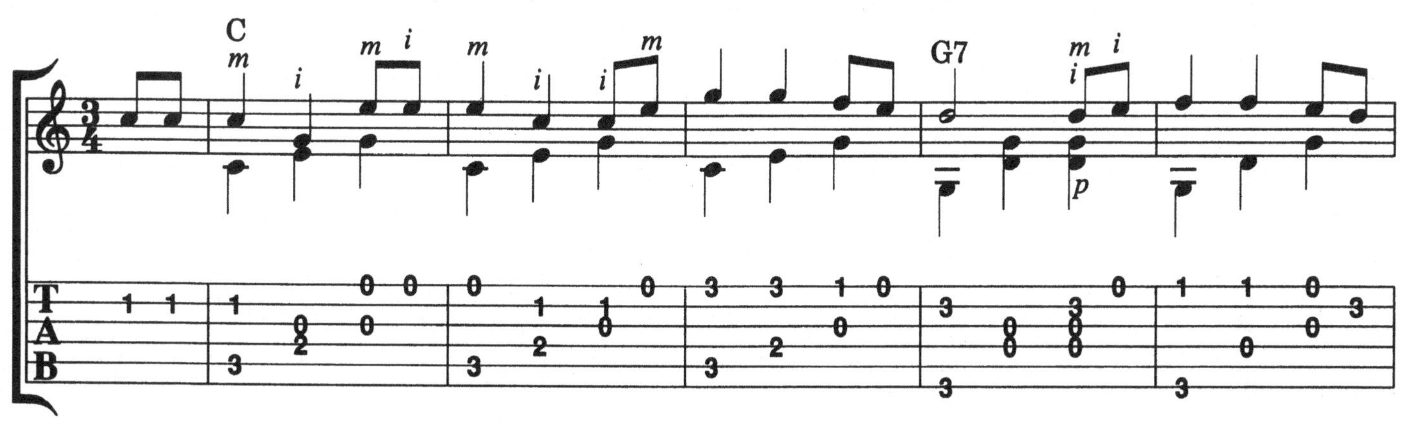

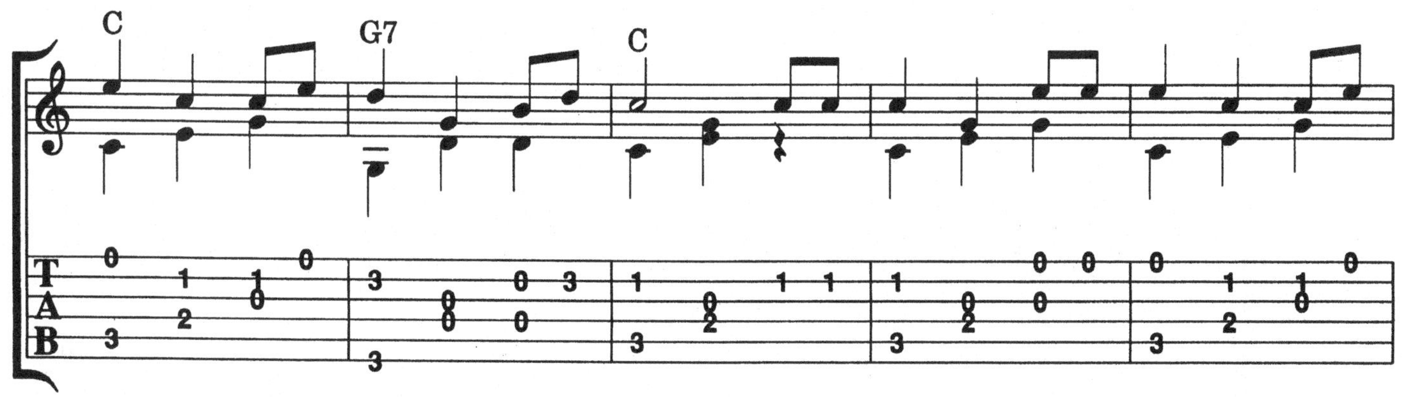

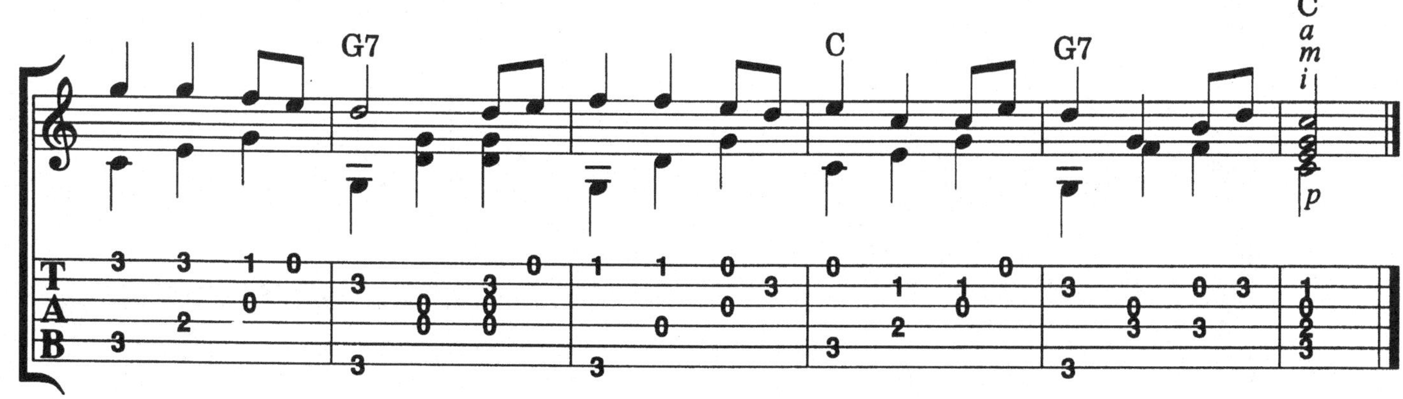

My Mountain Home

Two-Four Time

This sign indicates TWO-FOUR time.
2 -- beats per measure
4 -- a quarter note receives one beat.

TWO-FOUR time will have two beats per measure with the quarter note receiving one beat.

The Key of A Minor

(Relative to C Major)

Each Major key will have a Relative Minor key.

The Relative Minor Scale is built upon the *sixth tone* of the Major Scale.

The Key Signature of both will be the same.

The Minor Scale will have the same number of tones (7) as the Major.

The difference between the two scales is the arrangement of the whole-steps and half-steps.

There are *three forms* of the minor scale: 1. PURE or NATURAL, 2. HARMONIC, 3. MELODIC.

The A Minor Scale

Harmonic

The 7th tone is raised one half step ascending and descending.

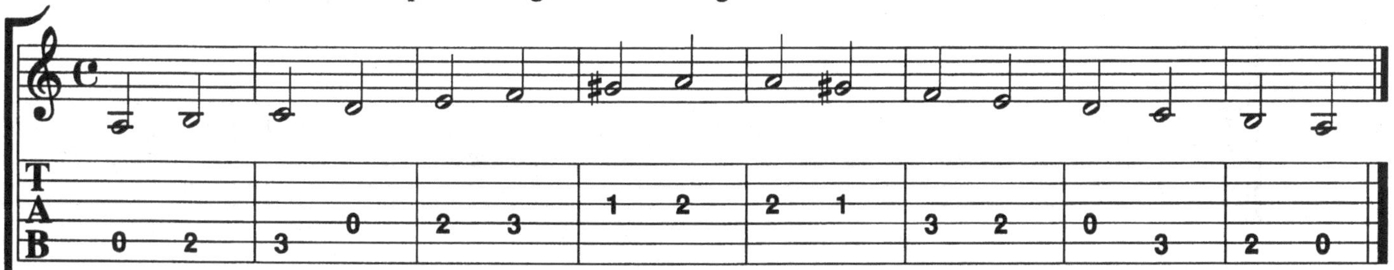

Melodic

The 6th & 7th tones are raised one half step ascending and lowered back to their normal pitch descending.

The Chords in the Key of A Minor

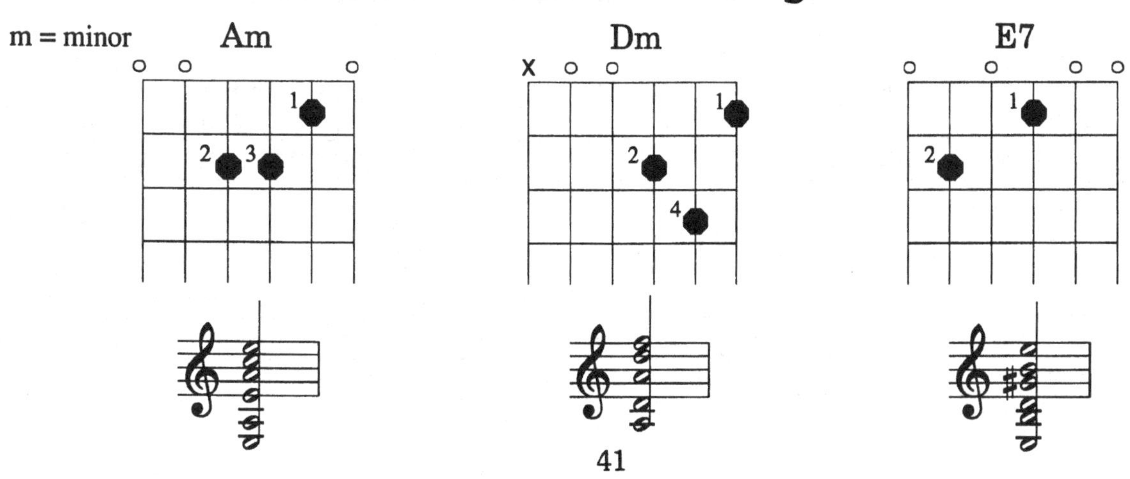

This sign ⁒ indicates that the previous measure is to be repeated.
In the following Study hold the chords as indicated, playing the melody from those chords.

Etude

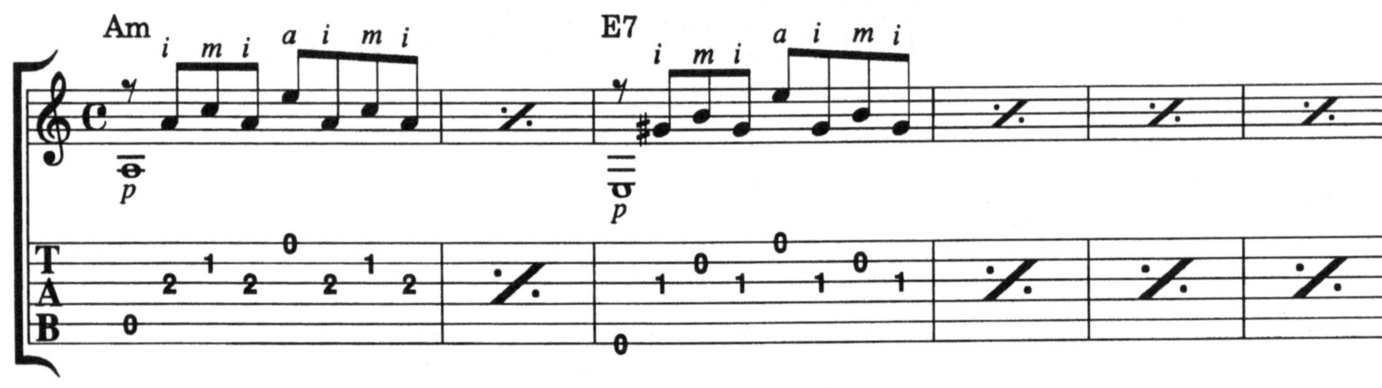

A Minor Study

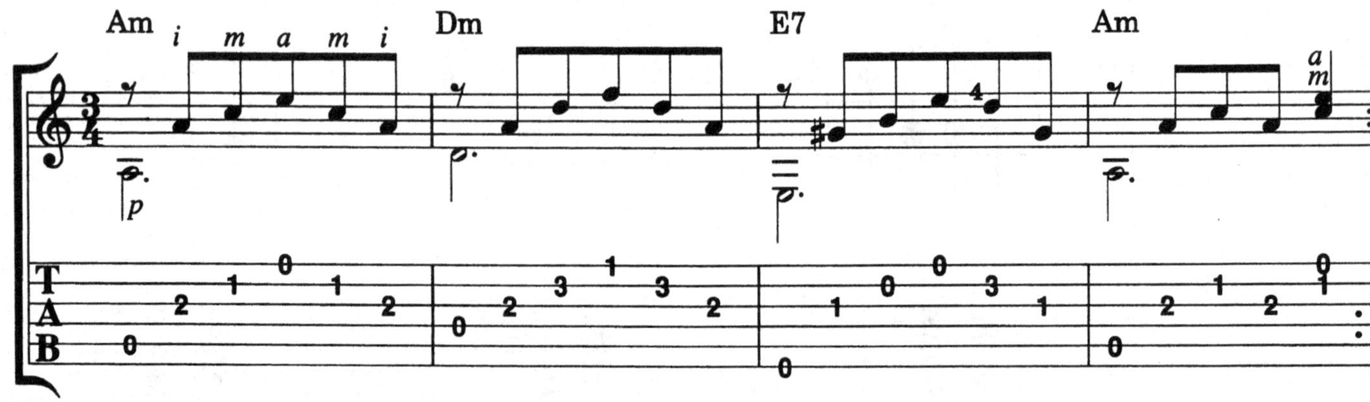

The Wayfarin' Stranger

* Use Am chord shown at top of page.

Dotted Quarter Notes

A DOT AFTER A NOTE increases its Value by ONE-HALF.

Dotted 1/4 - Note

Three Eighths

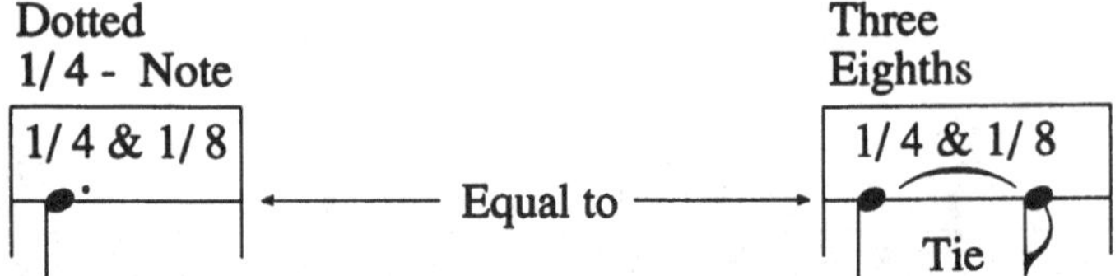

The count for the dotted quarter- note is as follows:

America the Beautiful

How to Count Triplets

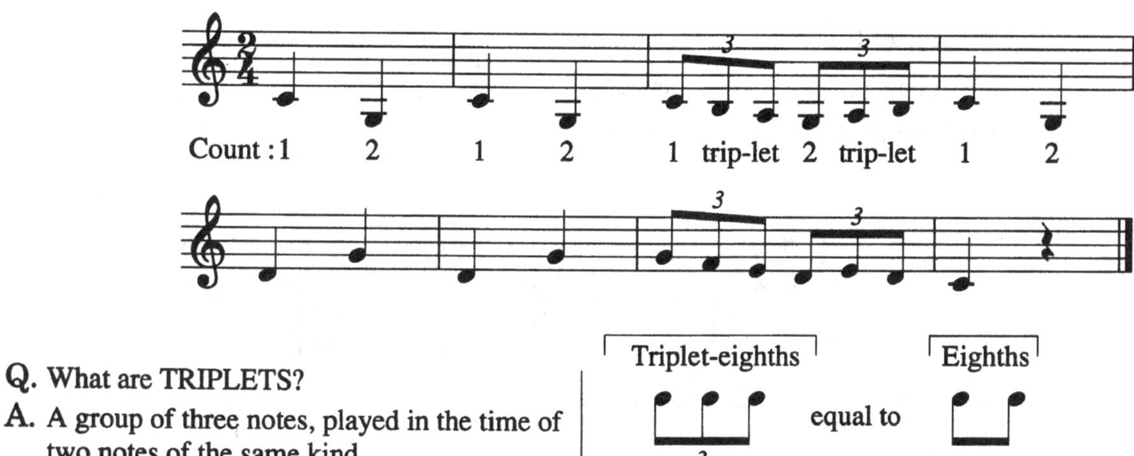

Q. What are TRIPLETS?

A. A group of three notes, played in the time of two notes of the same kind.

Triplets

p mi p mi p mi p mi

The Key of G

The Key of G will have one sharp. (F♯)
It will be identified by this signature:
The F-notes will be played as shown:

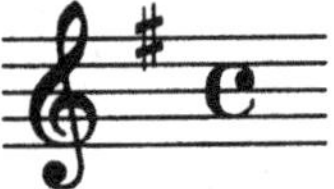

The G Scale

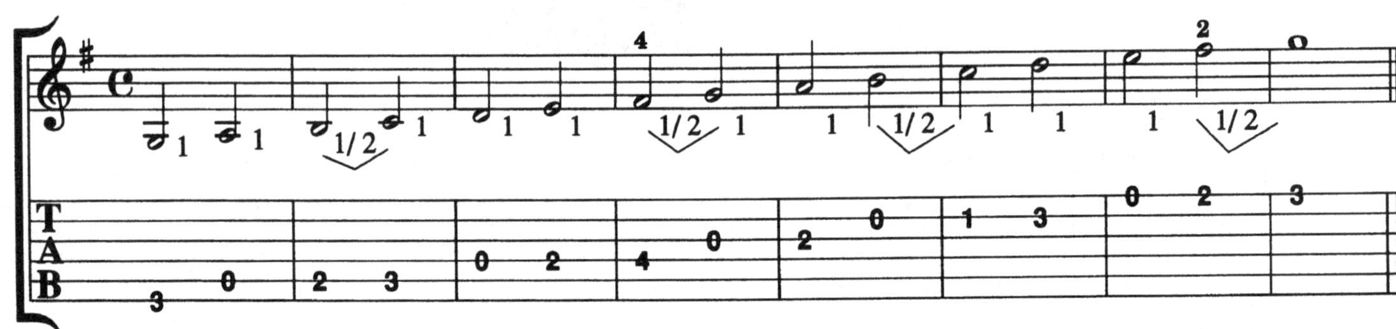

A Scale Study

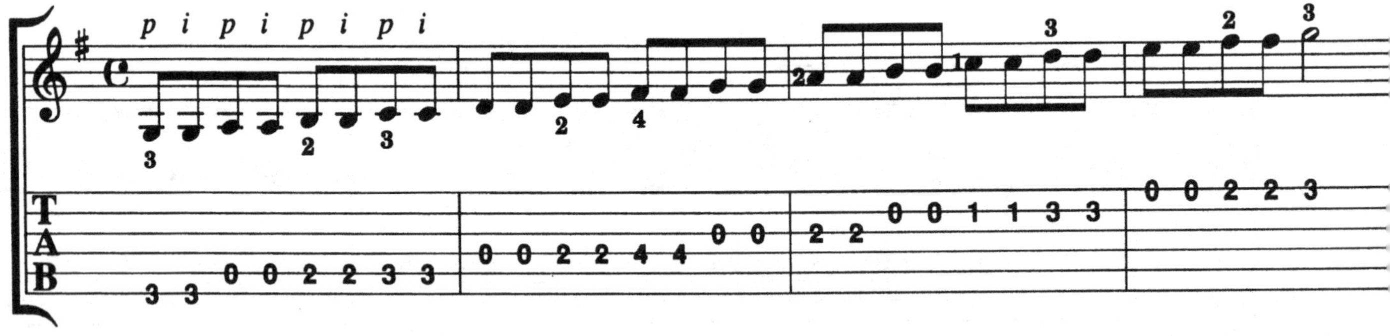

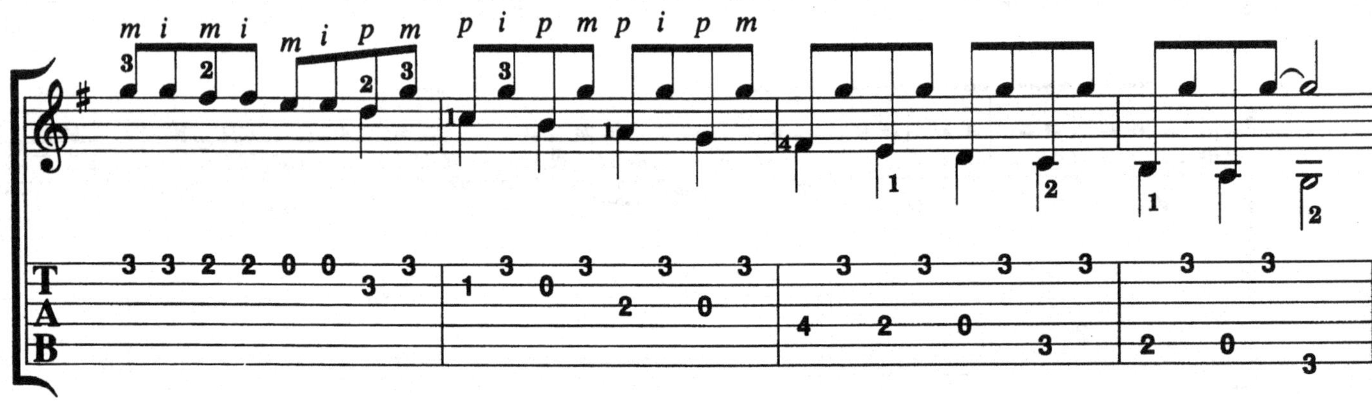

Three in One

m i m i m i m i m i m i
3 3 3 3 3 3 3 3 3 3 3 3
p p p p p p
T
A
B

p m i p m i p
p m i p m i p m i
T
A
B

T
A
B

T
A
B

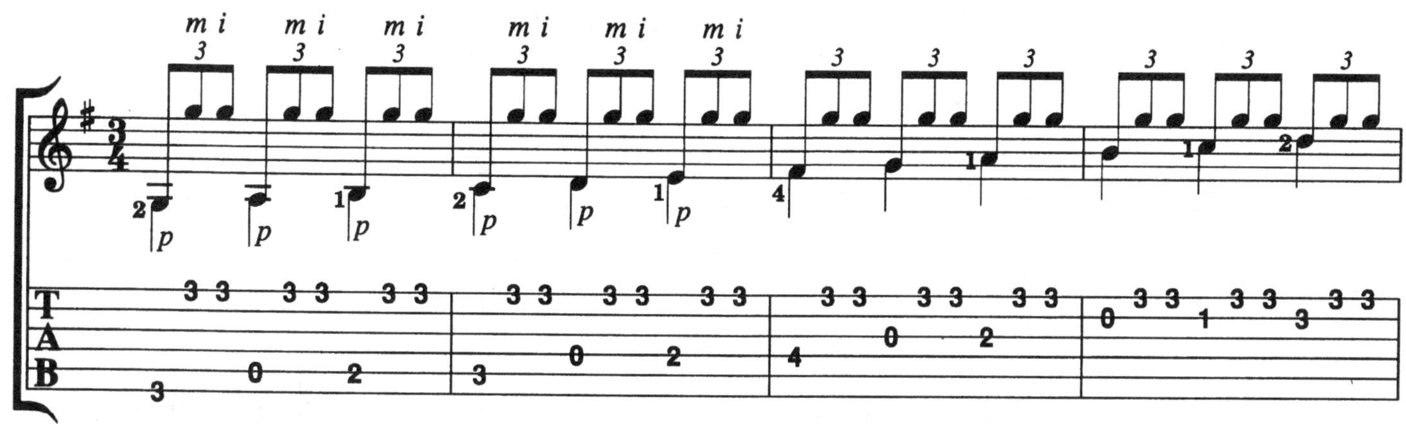

Chords in the Key of G

The chords in the key of G are.. G, C, and D7.

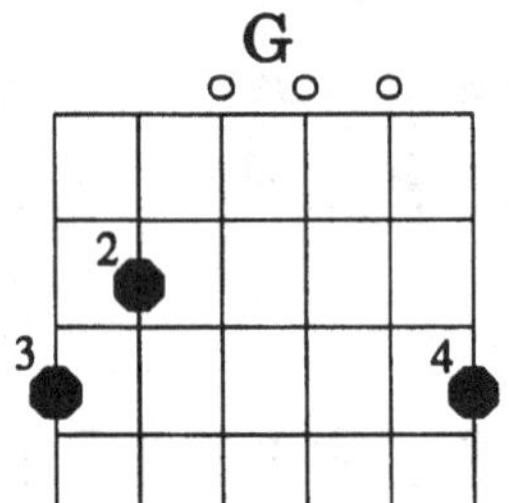

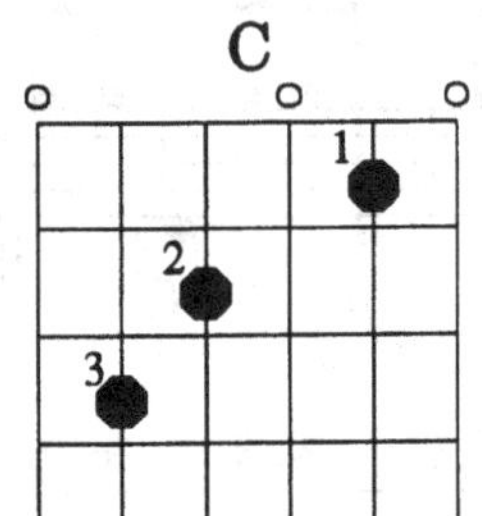

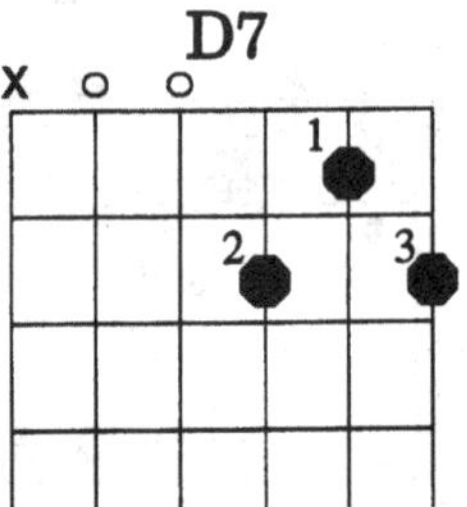

Accompaniment Styles in the Key of G

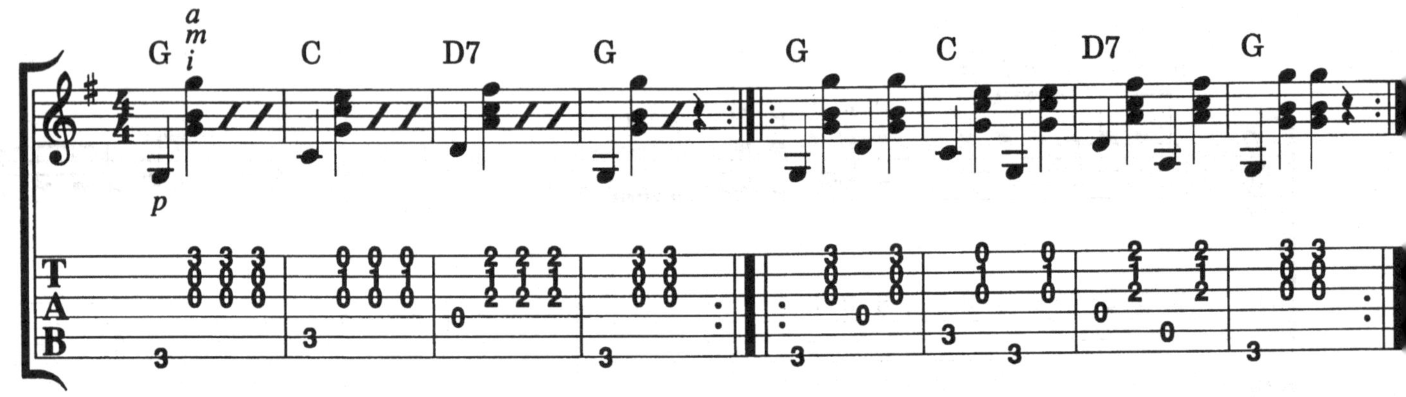

Old Folks at Home

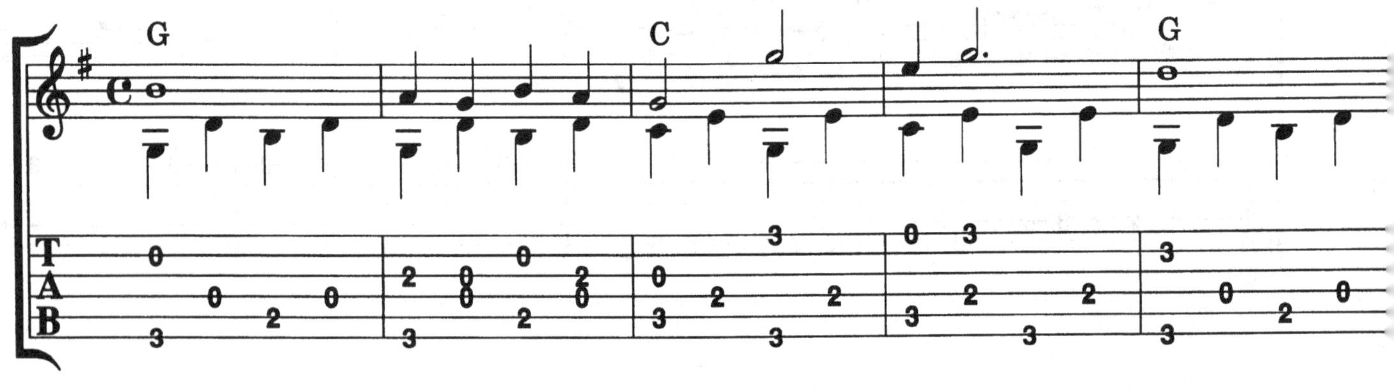

C
G
D9
G
D7
*
D9
G
C
G
D9
G
C
C
G
D9
G
3 Fret
D7

Home on the Range

Red River Valley

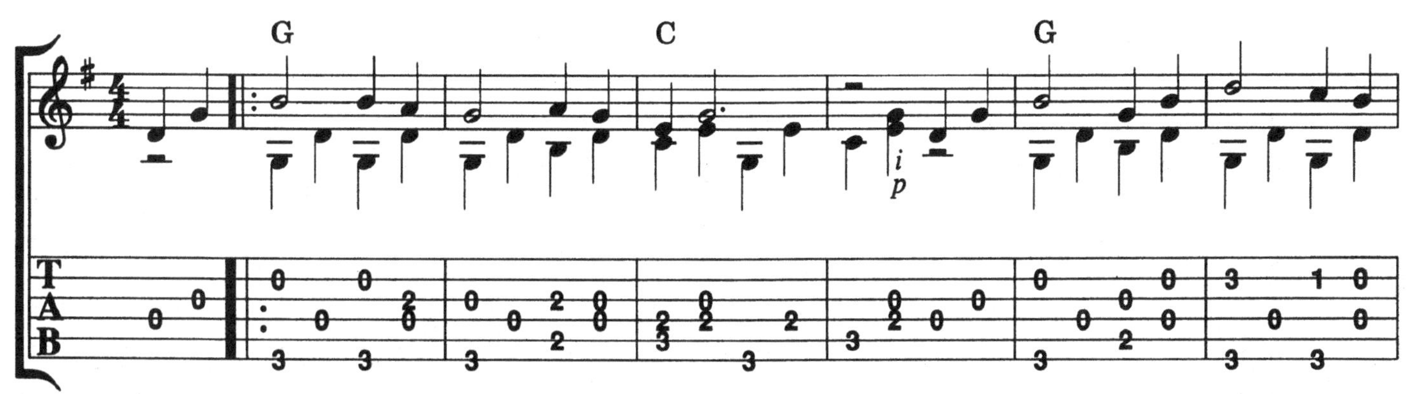

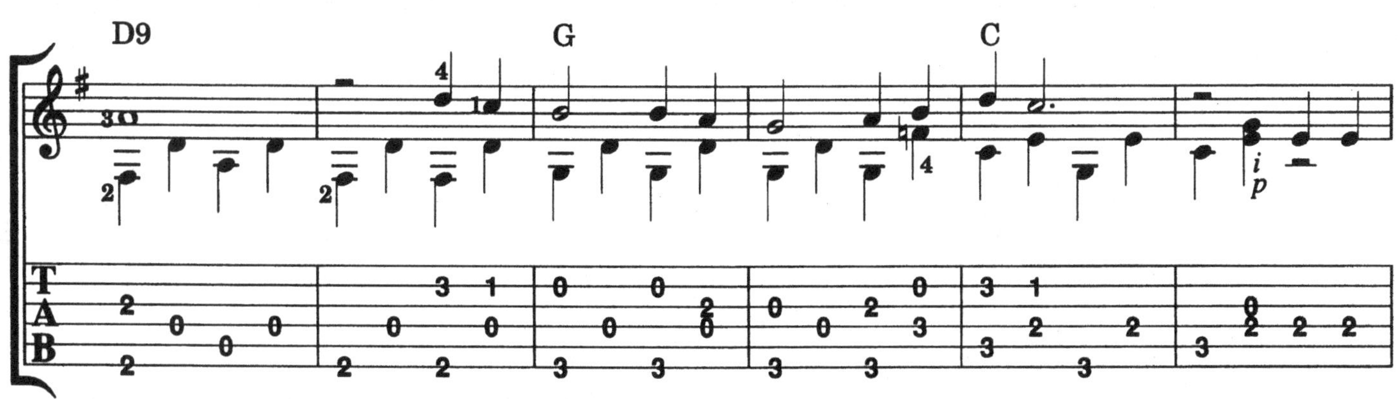

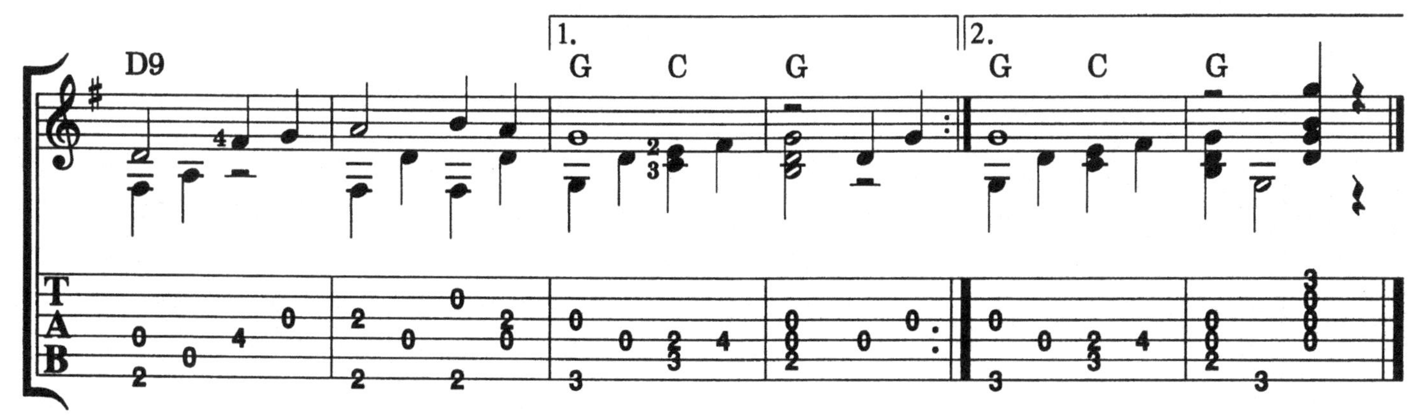

The Key of E Minor
(Relative to G Major)

The Key of E Minor will have the same key signature as G Major.

Two E Minor Scales

The Chords in the Key of E Minor

The Chords in the Key of E Minor are Em, Am, and B7.

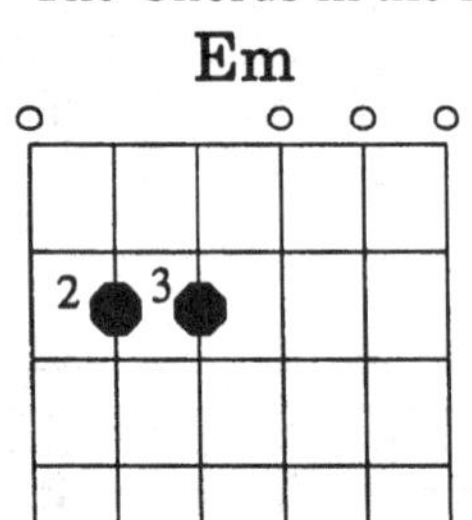

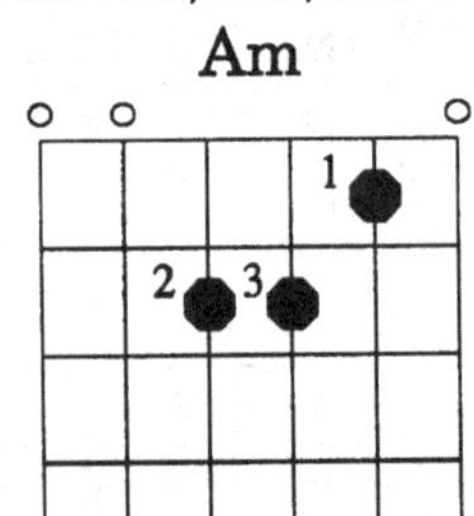

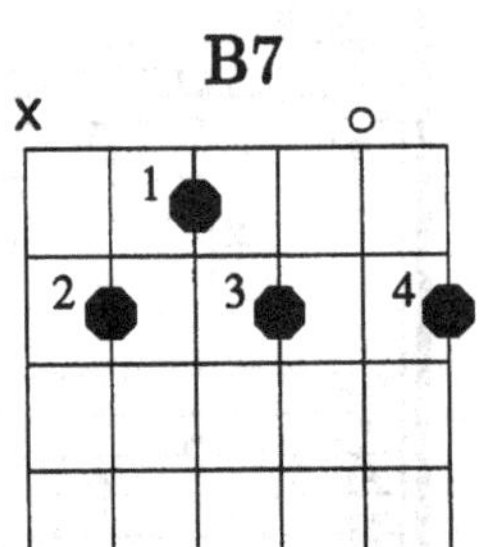

Accompaniment Styles in the Key of E Minor

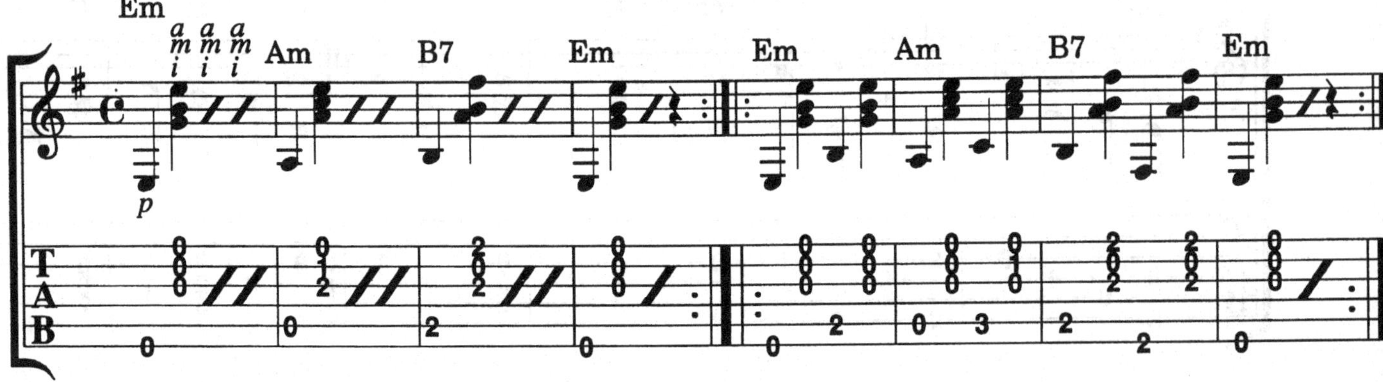

Waltz in E Minor

* B note ③ string fourth fret.

The Key of F

The Key of F will have one flat. All B-notes will be played one half-step lower as shown.

The F Major Scale

(Two Octaves)

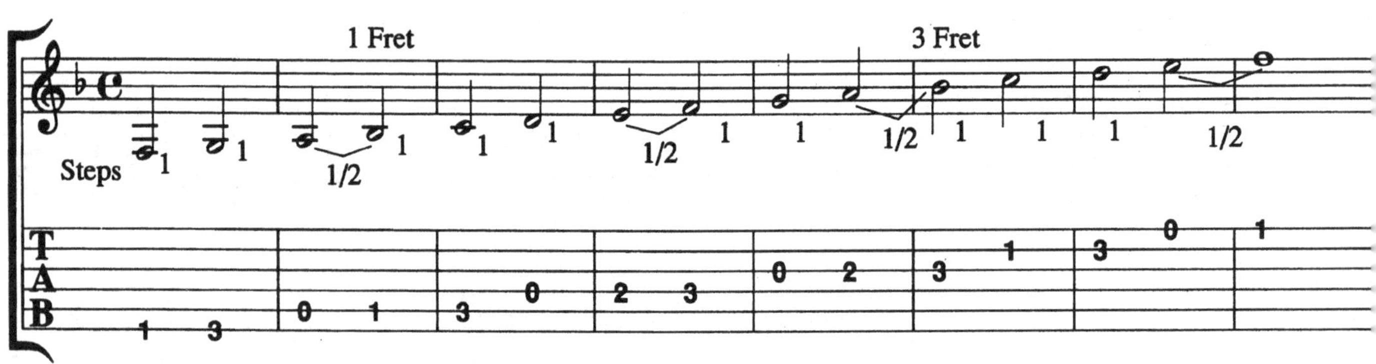

Triplet Etude

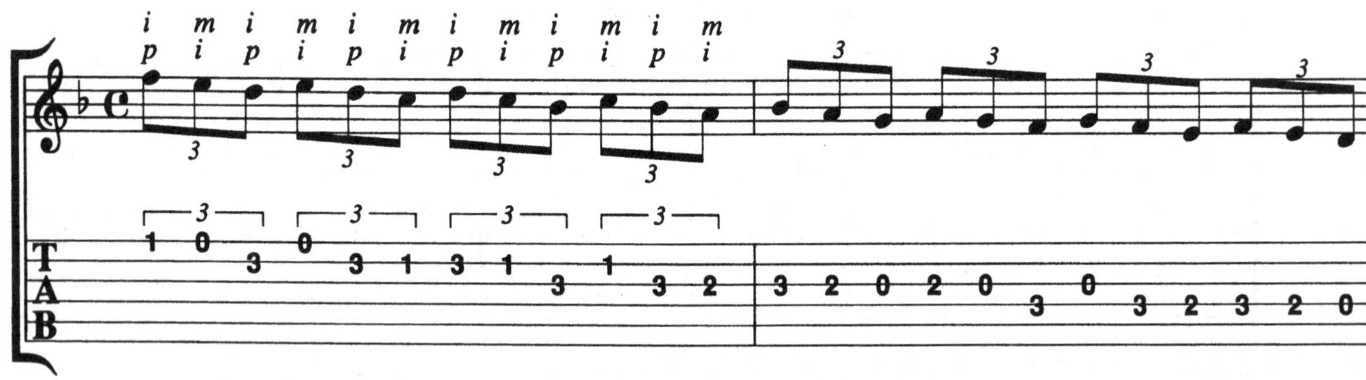

The Chords in the Key of F

The three chords in the key of F are F, B-flat, and C7.

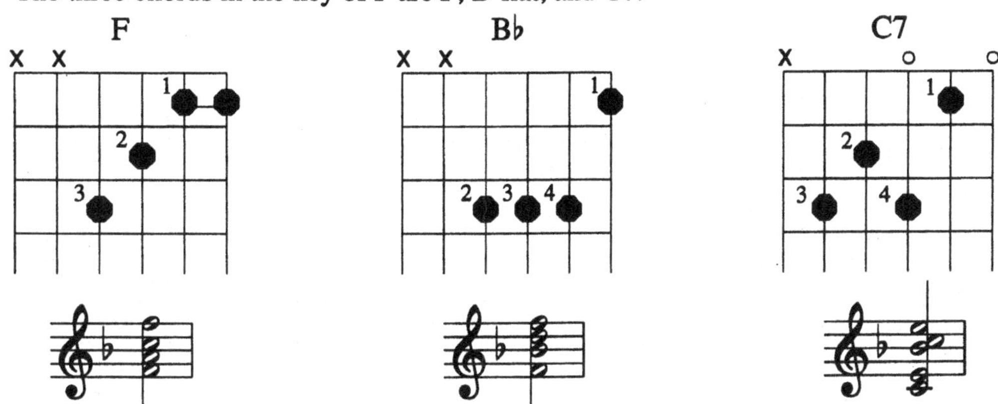

Accompaniment Styles

Common Time

May

Fine

D.C. al Fine

March Majestic

Sixteenth-Notes

In common time four sixteenth-notes equal one quarter-note.

They may be counted in this manner:
1-six-teenth-notes, 2-six-teenth-notes, 3-six-teenth-notes, 4-six-teenth-notes.

Example

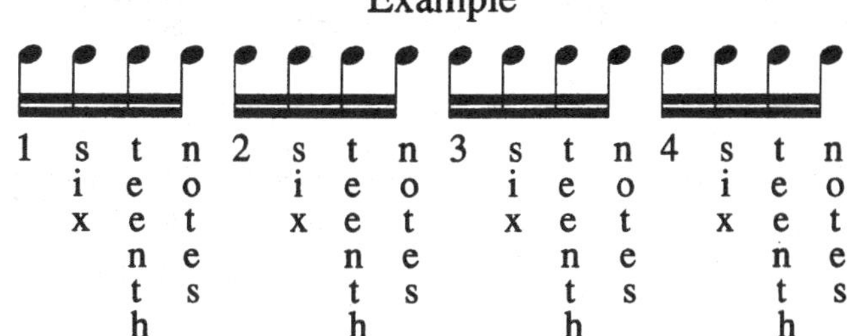

Table of Notes and Rests

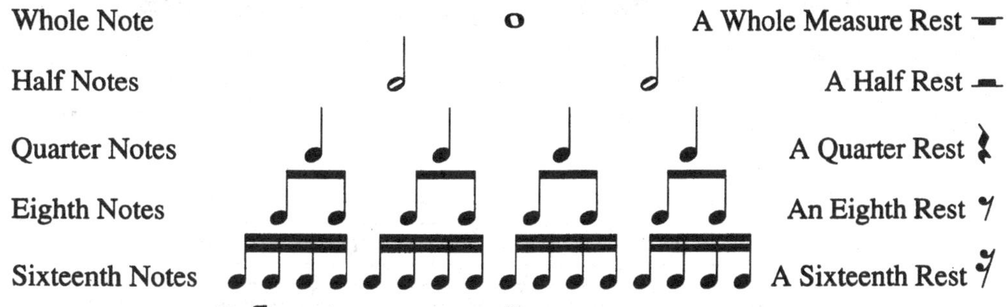

Sixteenth-Notes

Slowly at first

p a m i p a m i p a m i p a m i

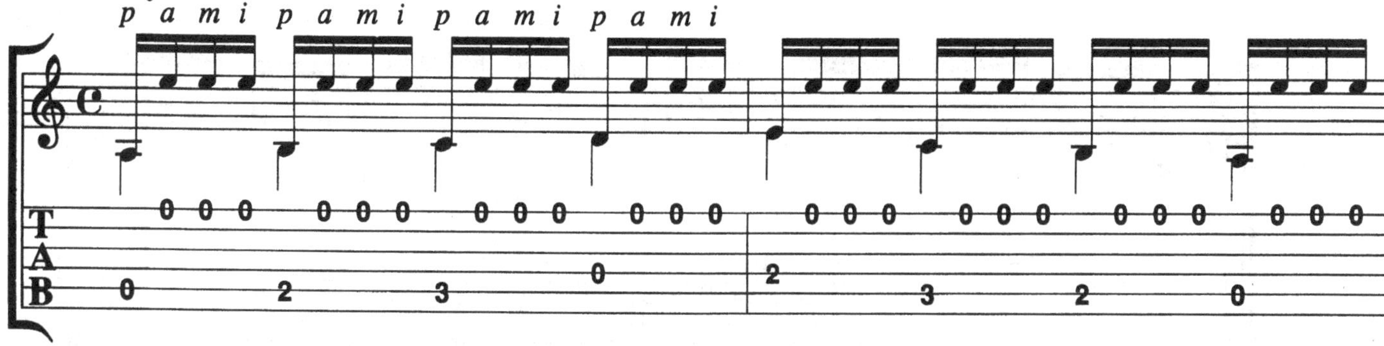

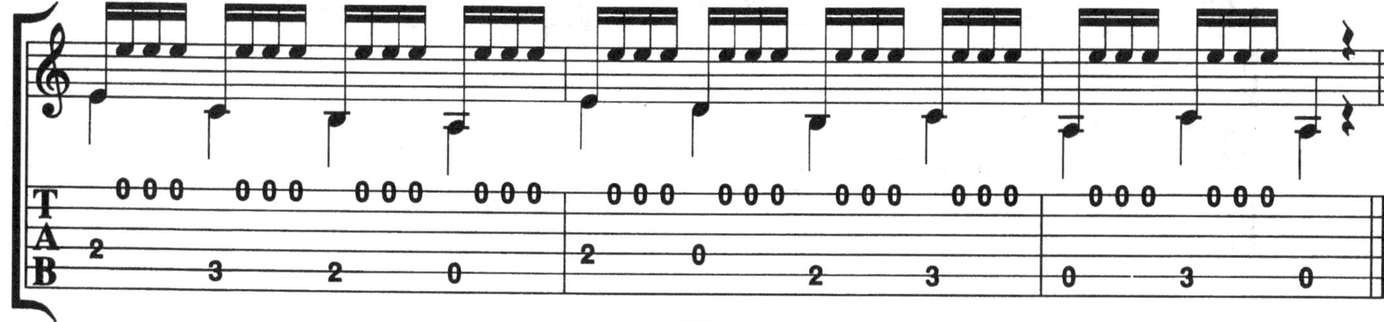

Prelude

Single String Sixteenths

The Notes on the Second String

Shown below are the notes on the second string.

Any note played upon the first string may be played upon the second string *five frets higher* than its location on the first string.

In the following diagram you will see the notes on the first string and directly below the same notes as played upon the second string. This is a very good aid in remembering the notes on the second string.

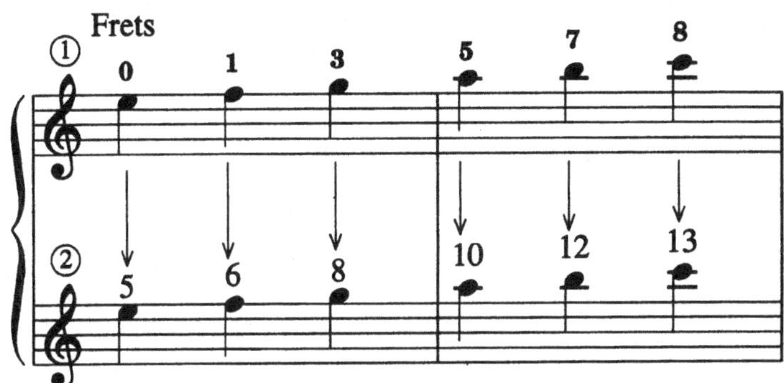

The C Scale in Thirds

The following study should be played upon the first and second string.

The *top-note will be on the first string* and the *bottom-note on the second.*

To facilitate execution, it is better to let the fingers remain upon strings as much as possible, gliding from fret to fret.

Carefully observe the fingering.

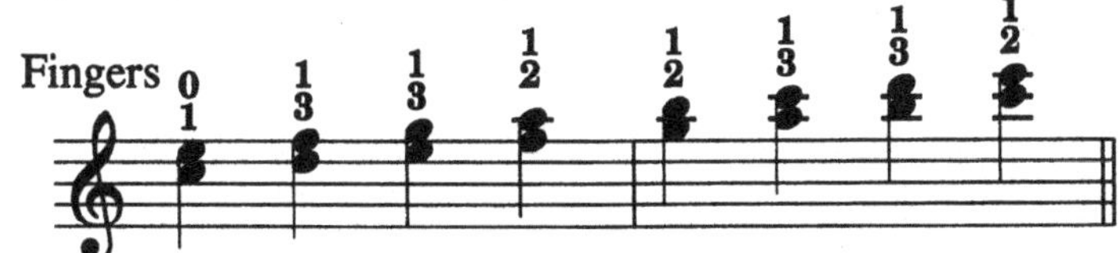

Notes on the Fifth Fret

The Key of D Minor
(Relative to F Major)
The D Minor Scales

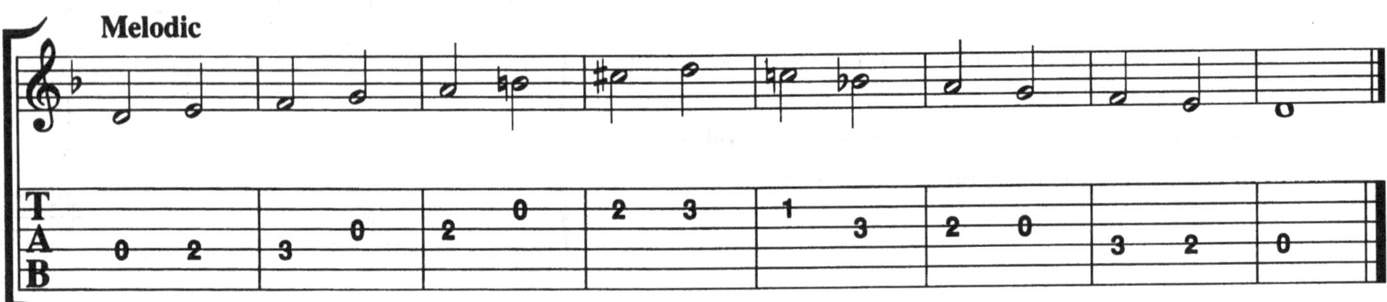

The Chords in the Key of D Minor

The three principal chords in the key of D minor are:

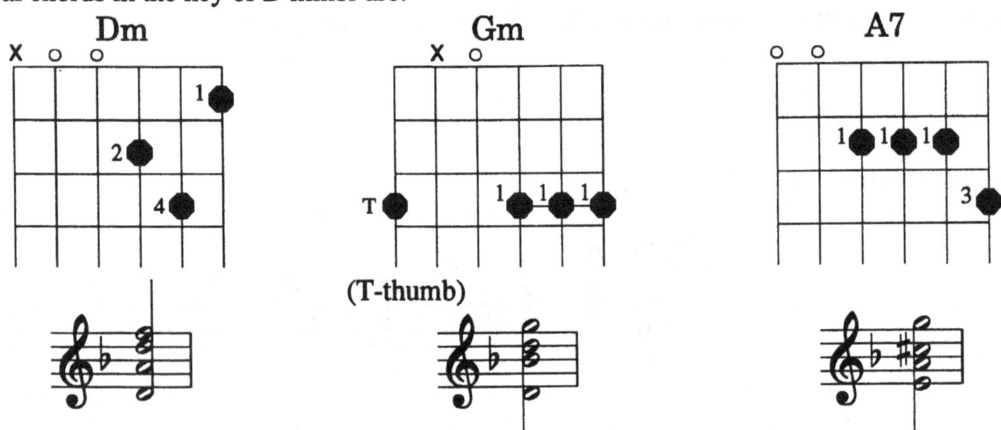

Accompaniment Styles
Common Time

Prelude in D Minor

Mist in the Valley

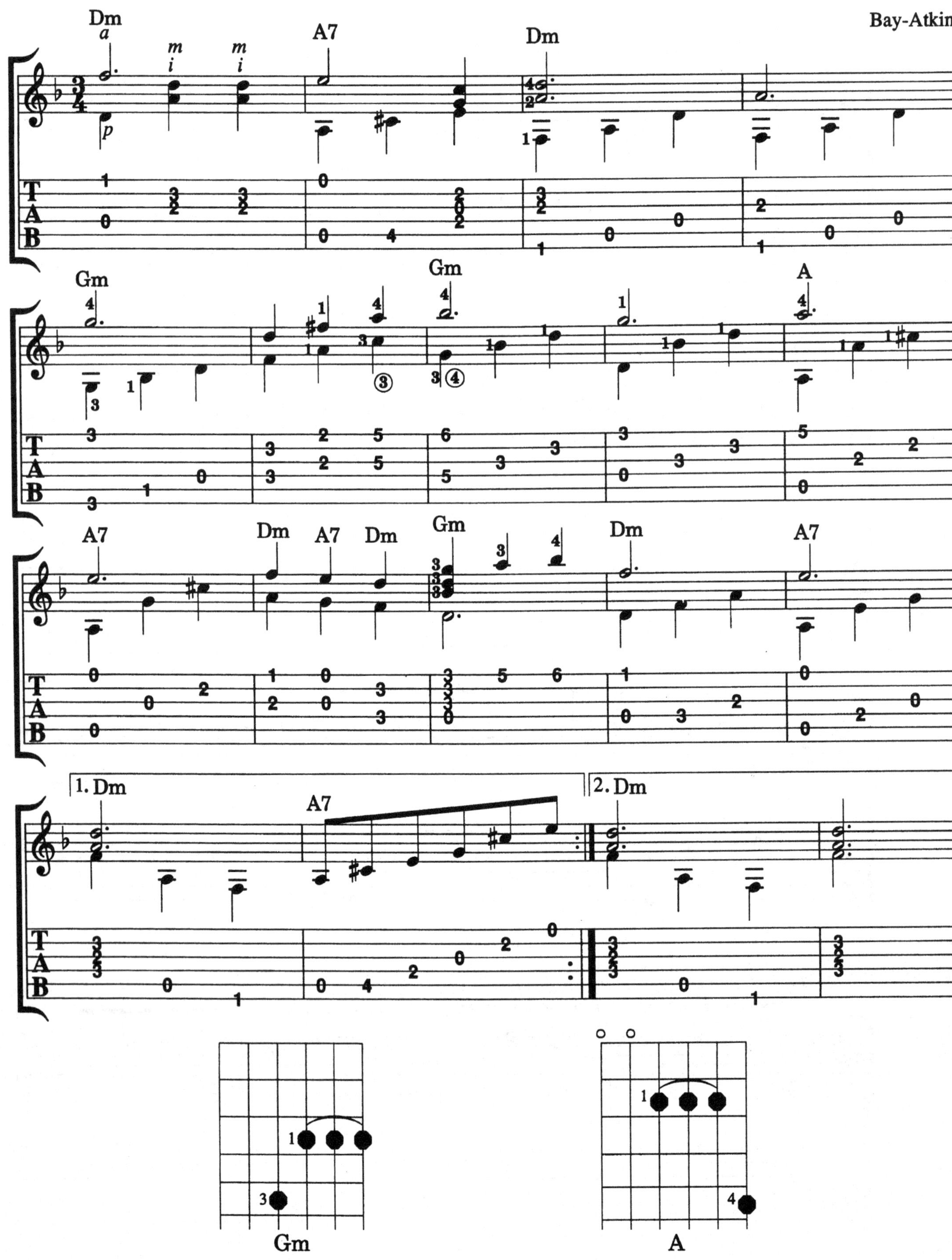

The Key of D Major

The Key of D Major will have two sharps-F♯ and C♯.
To facilitate the fingering in the Key of D Major, it is necessary to move the first finger to the second fret, the second finger to the third fret and the third finger to the fourth fret. (Note scale)

The D Major Scale

The Chords in the Key of D Major

The Chords in D Major are D, G and A7.

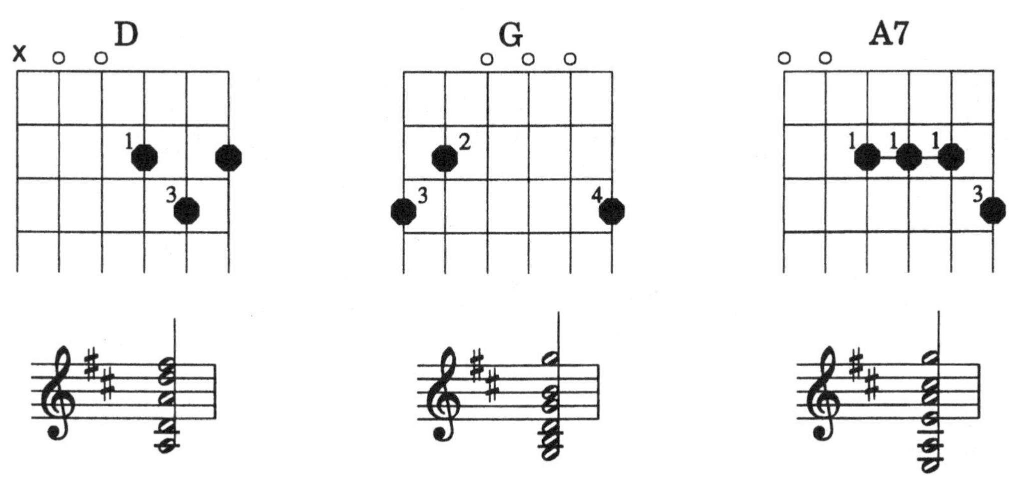

Accompaniment Styles

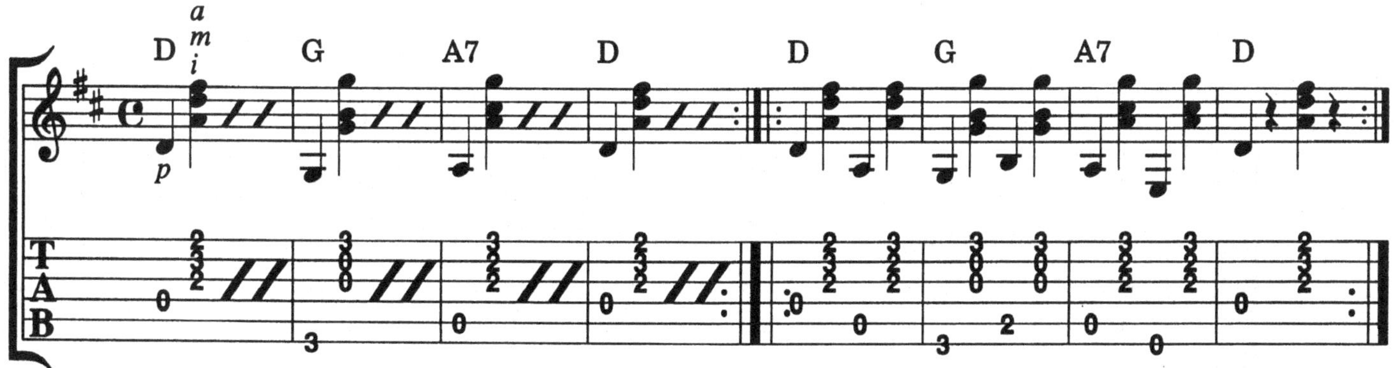

The D Scale in Two Octaves

The Streets of Laredo

Smoky Mountain Lullaby

Thirds in the Key of D

Drink to Me Only With Thine Eyes

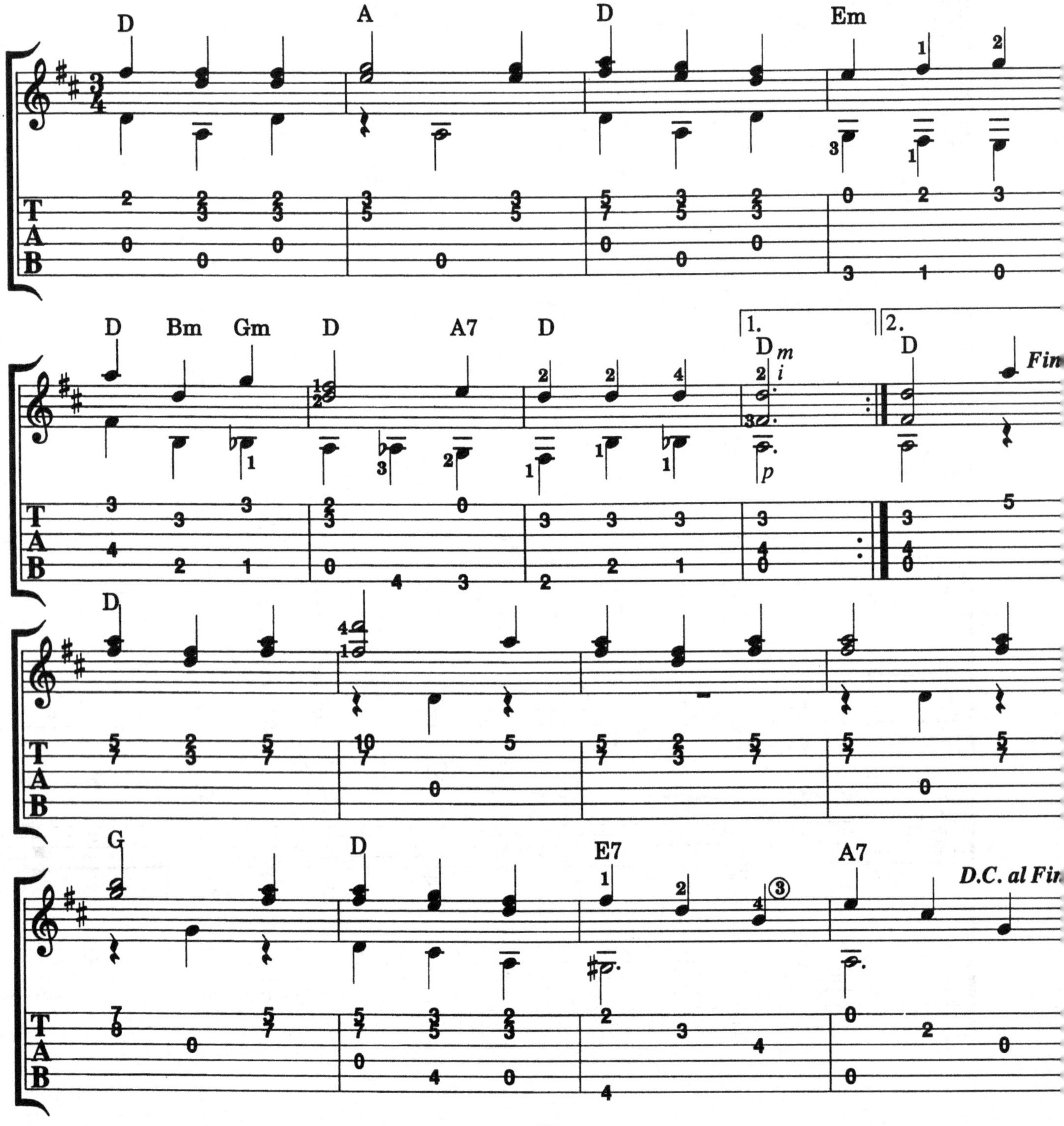

D A D Em

D Bm Gm D A7 D 1. D 2. D *Fine*

D

G D E7 A7 *D.C. al Fine*

The Key of B Minor

(Relative to D Major)

The B Minor Scales

Harmonic

Melodic

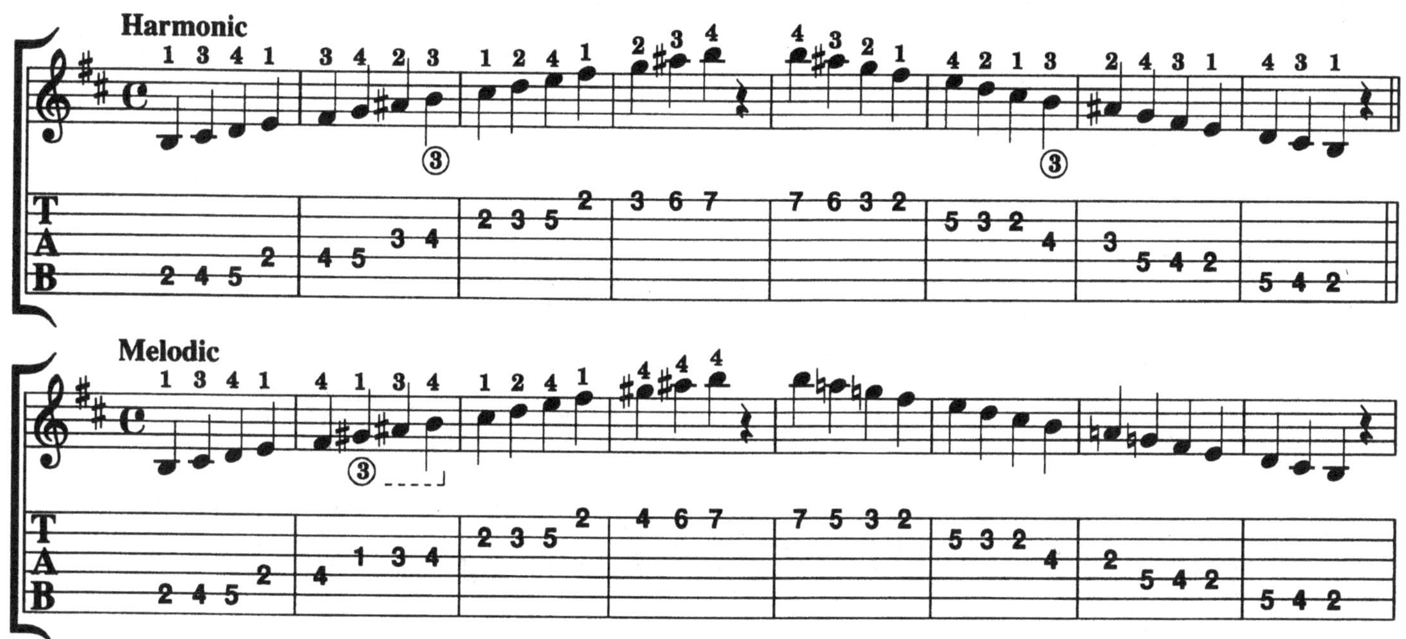

Etude in B Minor

Harmonic

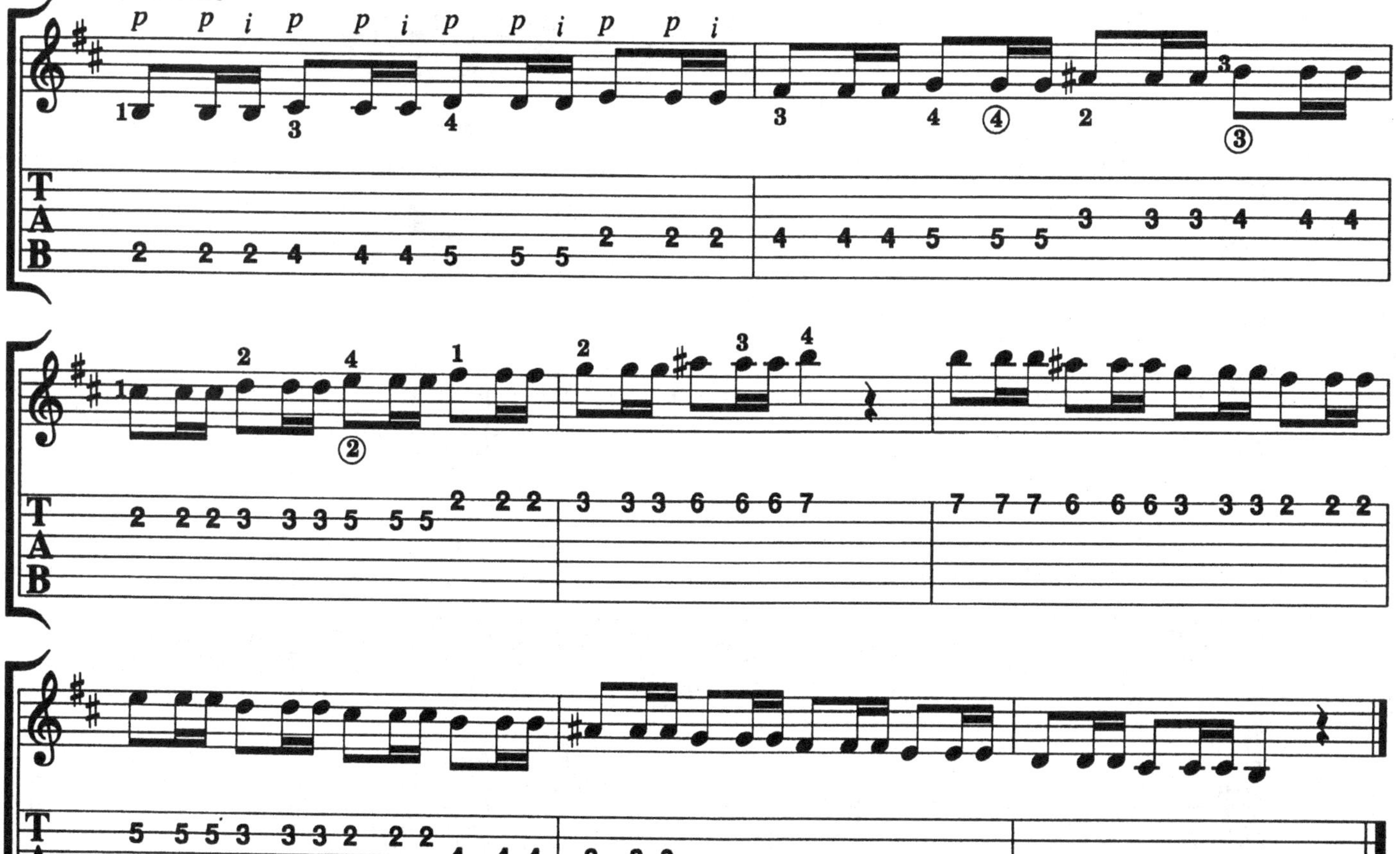

The Chords in the Key of B Minor

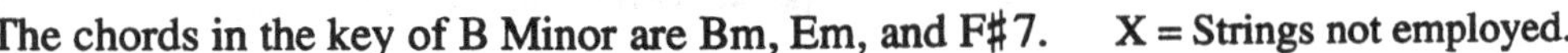
The chords in the key of B Minor are Bm, Em, and F♯7. X = Strings not employed.

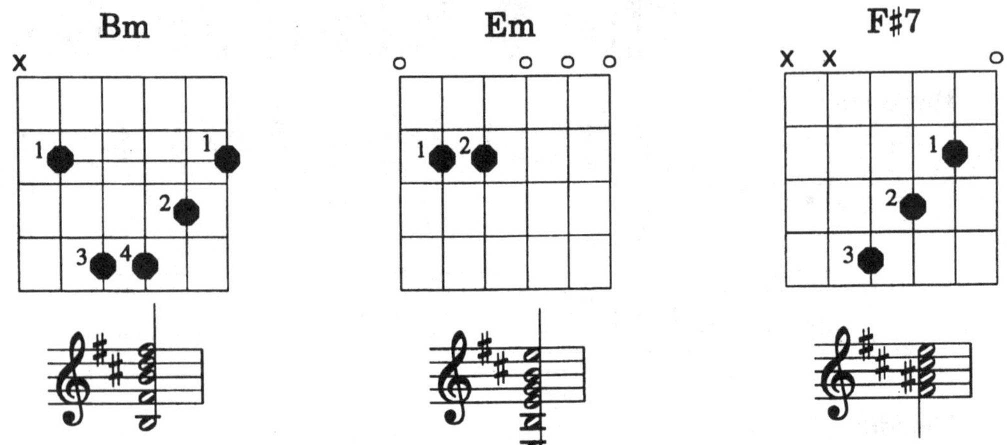

Accompaniment Styles

Southern Picking

Love Song

Etude

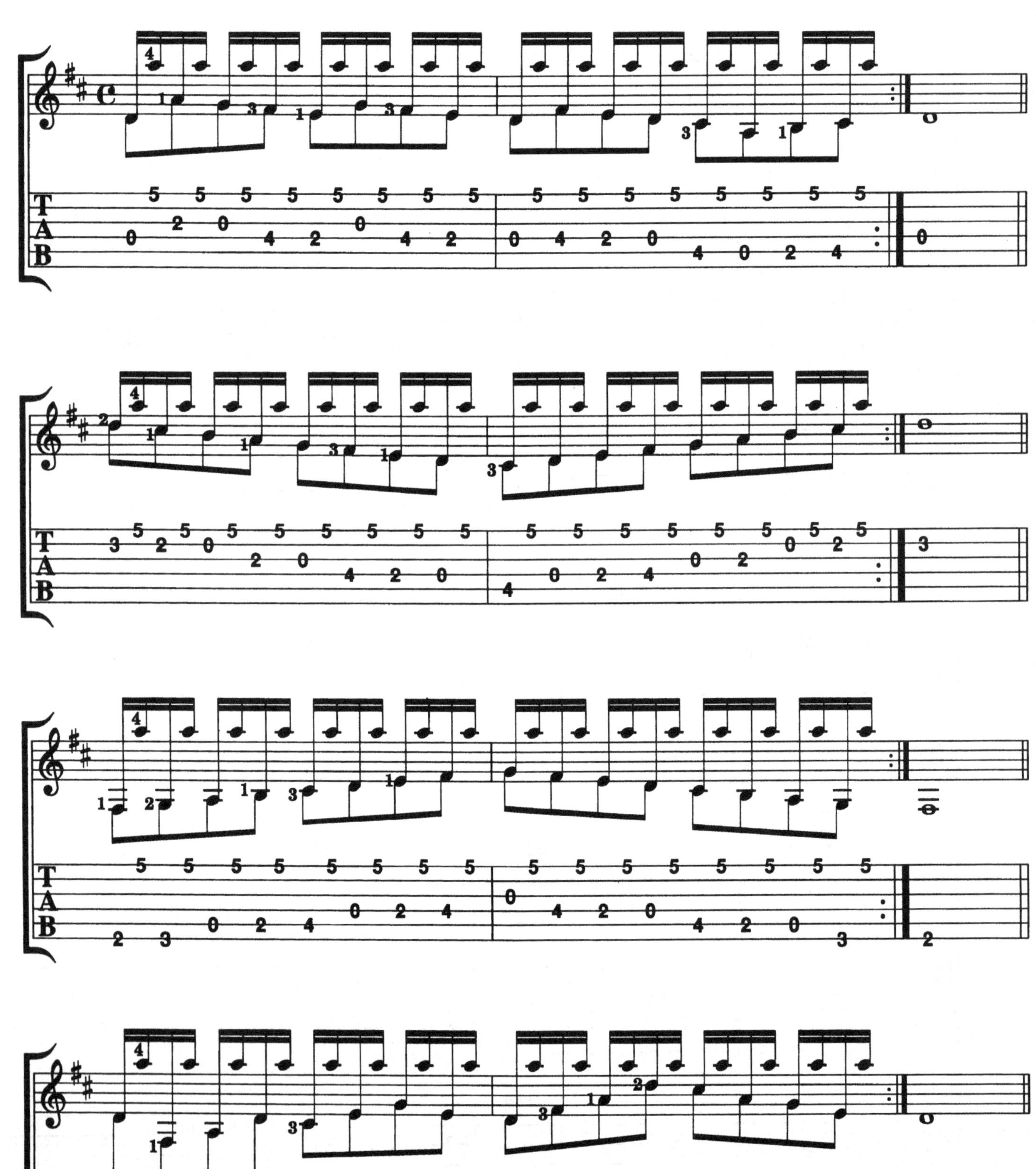

The Key of A

The key of A will have three sharps. (F♯, C♯, and G♯.)

It will be identified by this signature: 

The notes affected by the above signature will be played as shown:

Etude

The Chords in the Key of A

The three principal chords in the key of A are A, D, and E7.

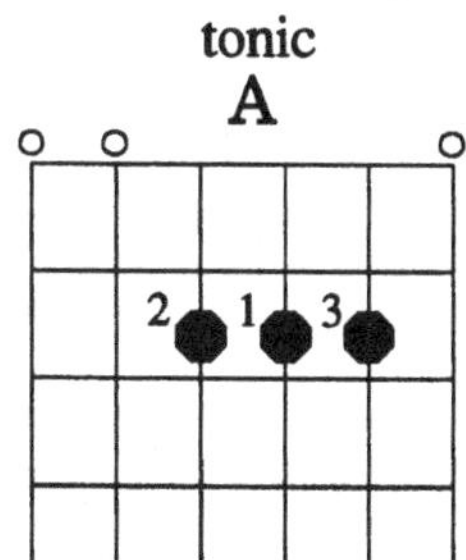

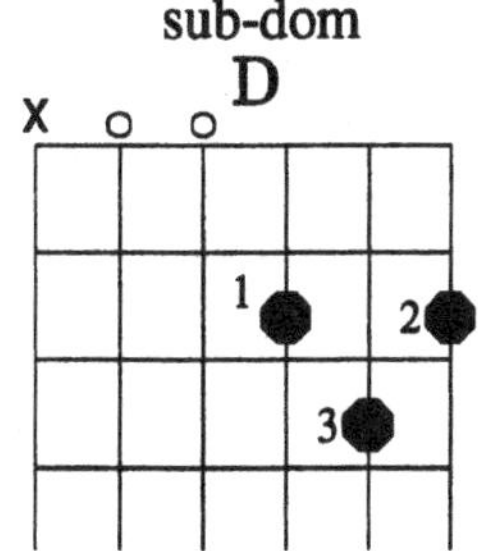

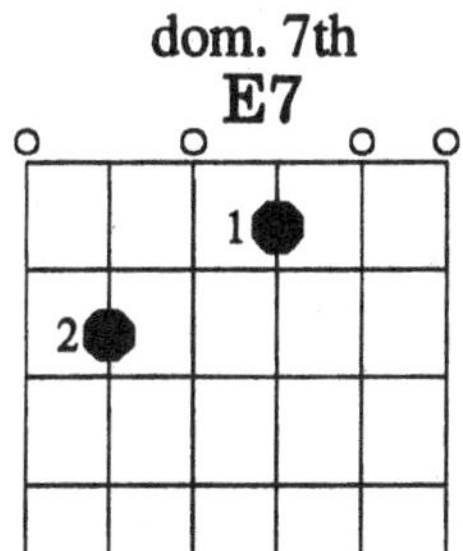

The Musical Notation of the Chords

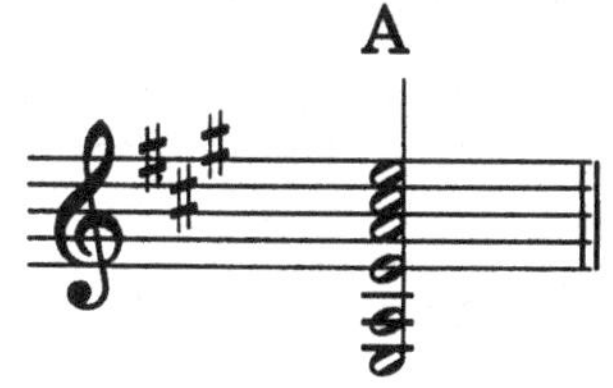

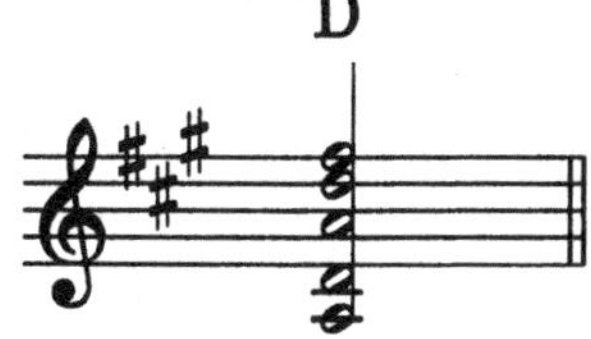

Accompaniment Styles

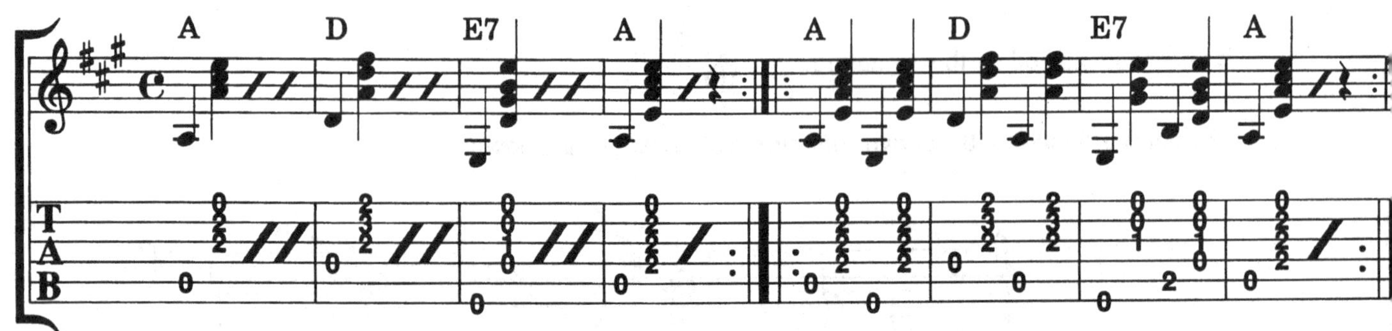

Six-Eight Time

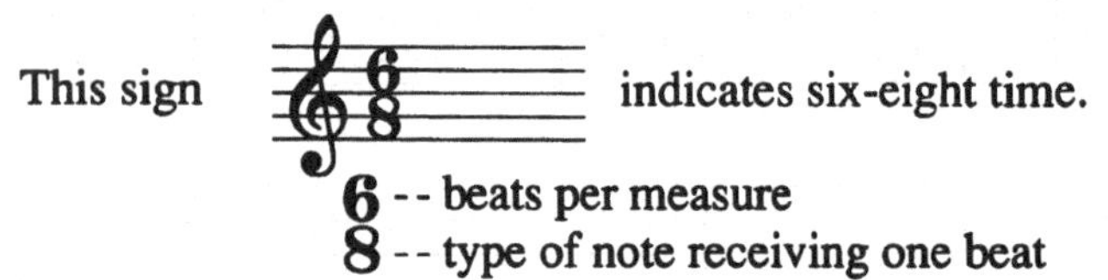

This sign indicates six-eight time.

6 -- beats per measure
8 -- type of note receiving one beat

An Eighth-note ♪ = one beat, a quarter-note ♩ = two beats and a dotted quarter-note ♩. = three beats, a sixteen - note 𝅘𝅥𝅯 = $\frac{1}{2}$ beat.

Six-eight time consists of two units containing three beats each.

It will be counted: ♩♩♩ ♩♩♩ with the accents on beats one and four.
1̲·2·3·4̲·5·6

The Carnival of Venice

The Notes on the Third String

The notes on the third (G) string are located as shown:

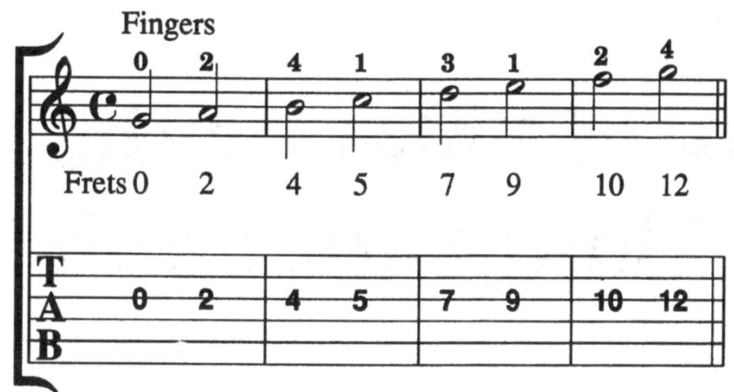

The G Scale

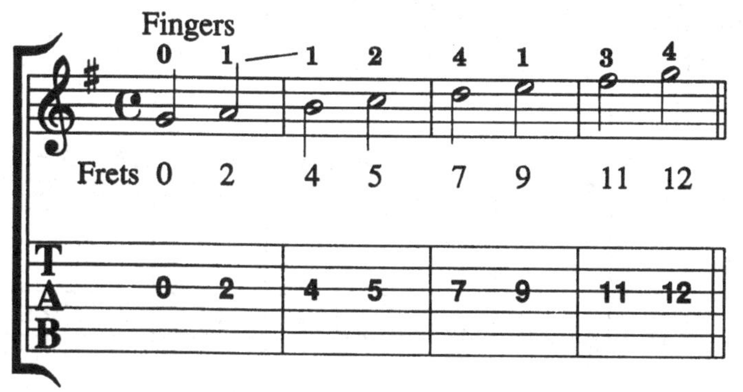

The A Scale

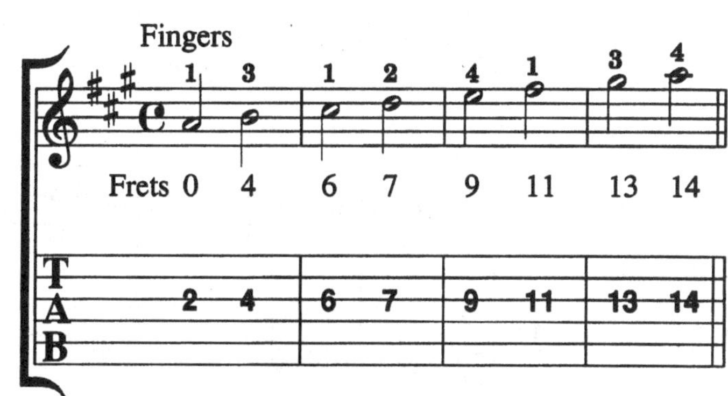

G String Etude

The Notes of the Fourth String

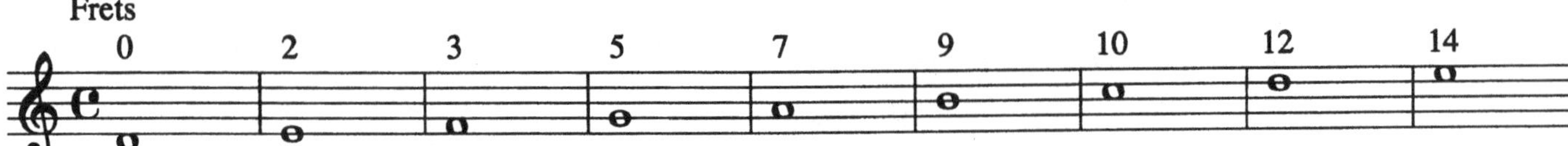

A Table of Notes on the First, Second, Third and Fourth Strings

It is important that the student thoroughly understands the above chart before proceeding.

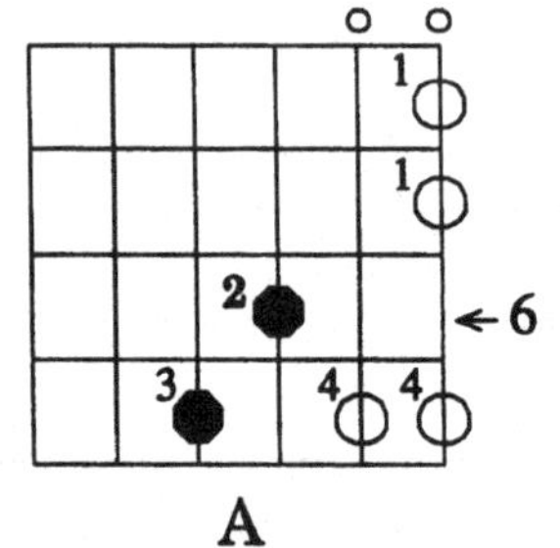

Chords used in the following solo. Circles indicate notes that may be used with or added to the chord.

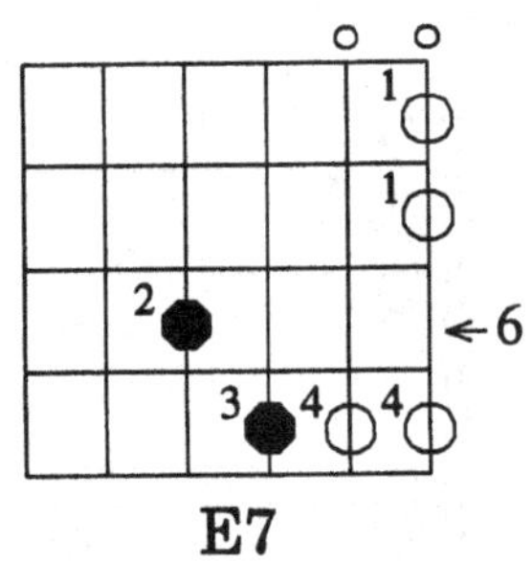

Smooth

Tenting Tonight

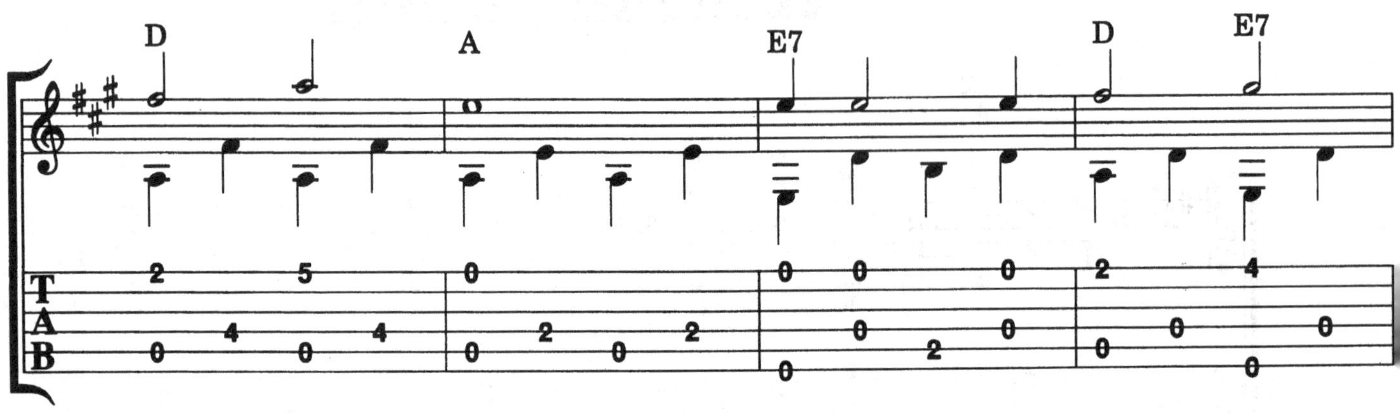

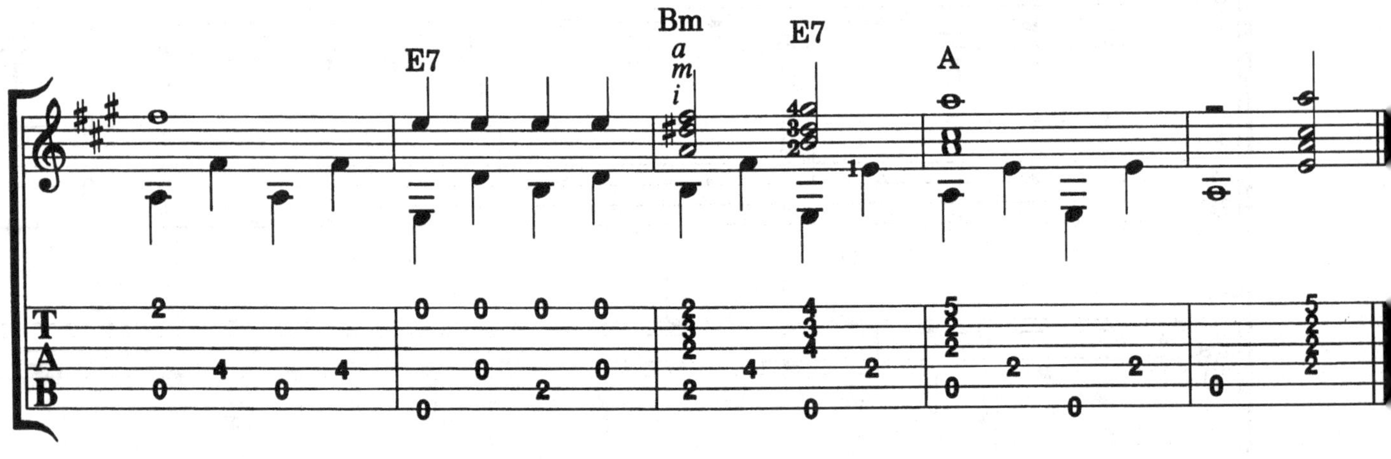

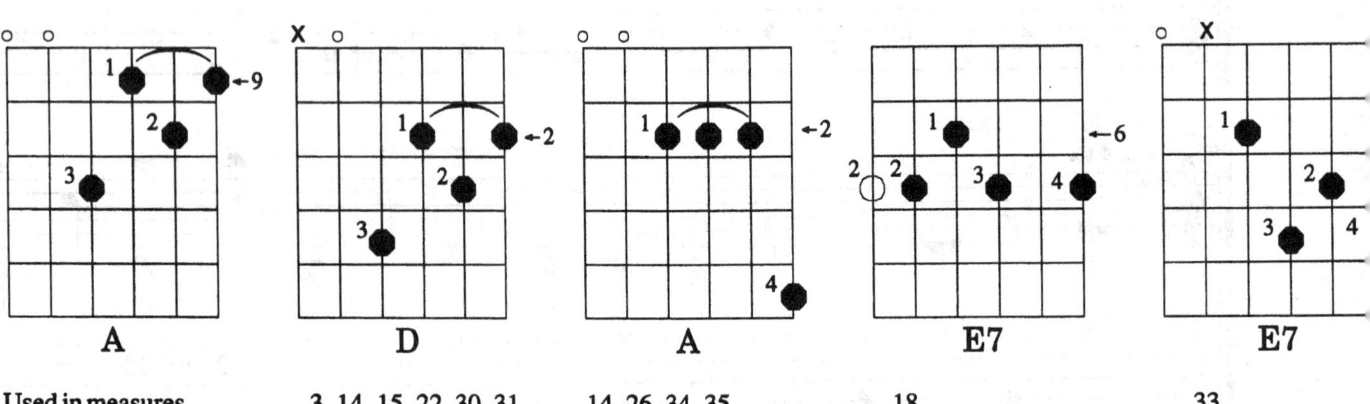

Used in measures 1, 2, 20, 21 | 3, 14, 15, 22, 30, 31 | 14, 26, 34, 35 | 18 | 33

The Key of F♯ Minor

(Relative to A Major)

Two F♯ Minor Scales

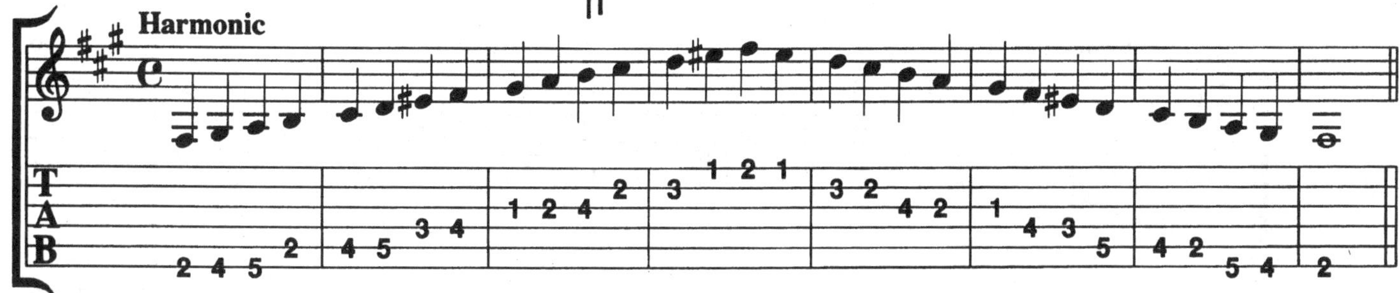

The Chords in the Key of F♯ Minor

The chords in the Key of F♯ Minor are F♯m, Bm, and C♯7.

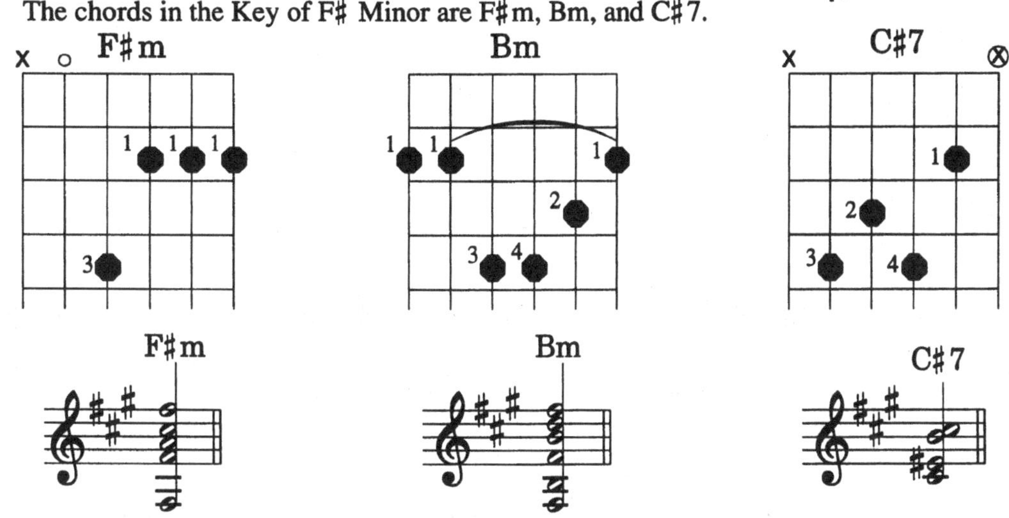

⊗ = DEADENED STRING–Kill the sound of the string with the unused part of the left hand.
(See the MEL BAY MELODY CHORD PLAYING SYSTEM for further explanation.)

Accompaniment Styles

The Key of E Major

The key of E will have four sharps. All F, C, G, and D notes will be sharped.

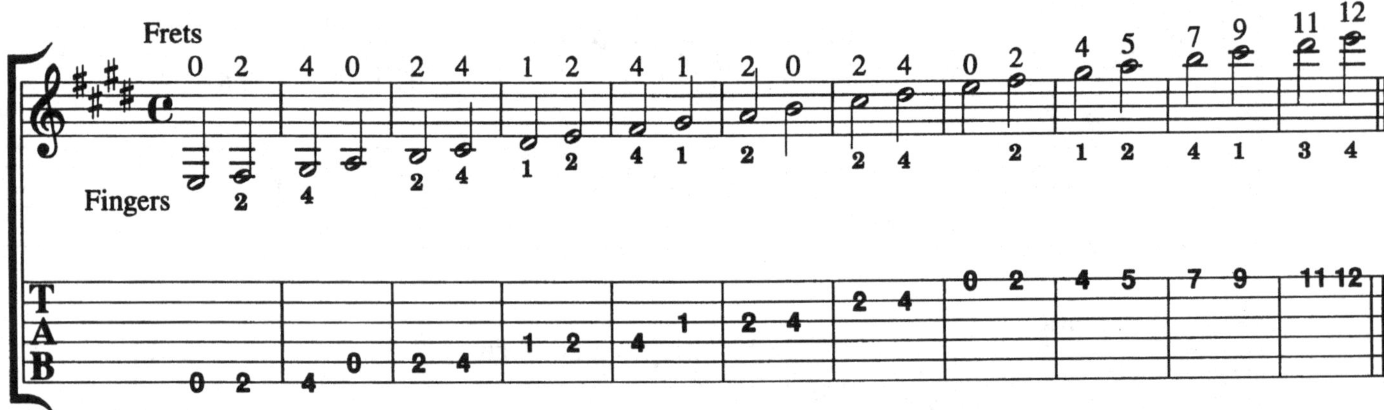

The Chords in the Key of E Major

The Chords in the Key of E Major are E, A, and B7

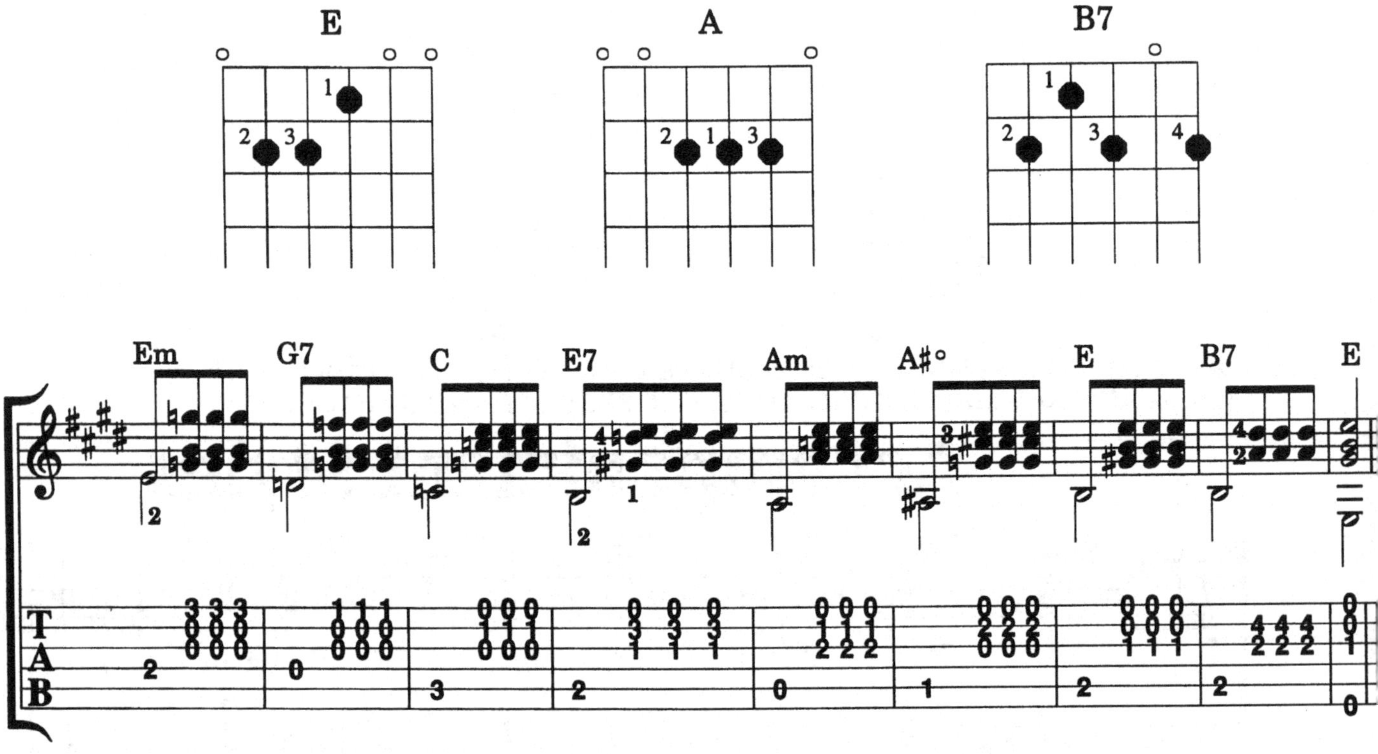

Careless Love

More Chromatic Signs

Up to this point we have studied and used the Sharp (♯), the Flat (♭), and the Natural (♮).
The student is familiar by now with their function. We now introduce the Double-Sharp and the Double-Flat.

𝄪 = Double-Sharp. A Double-Sharp will raise the sound of a tone *two frets.*

𝄫 = Double Flat. A Double-Flat will lower the sound of a tone *two frets.*

A natural will cancel all sharps, flats, double-sharps and double-flats. If a note has been double-sharped or double flatted, the return to one sharp or flat will require a natural sign followed by the desired sharp or flat.

Example

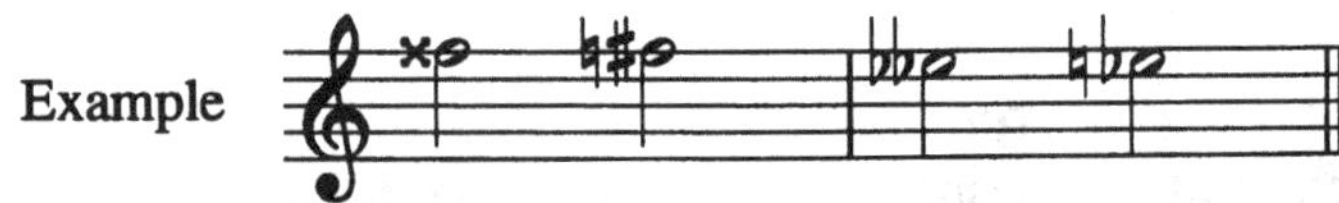

Ode to Bob

Mel Bay

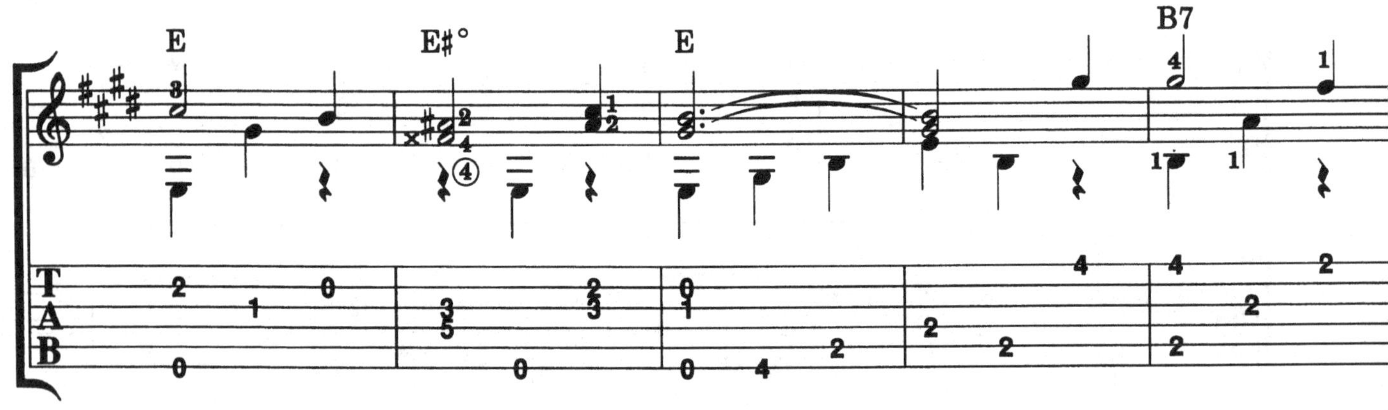

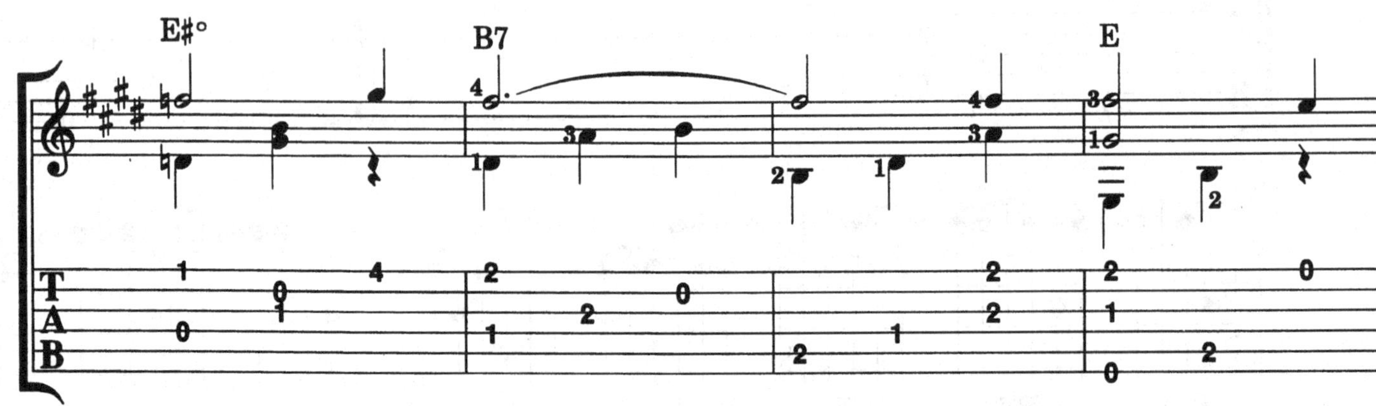

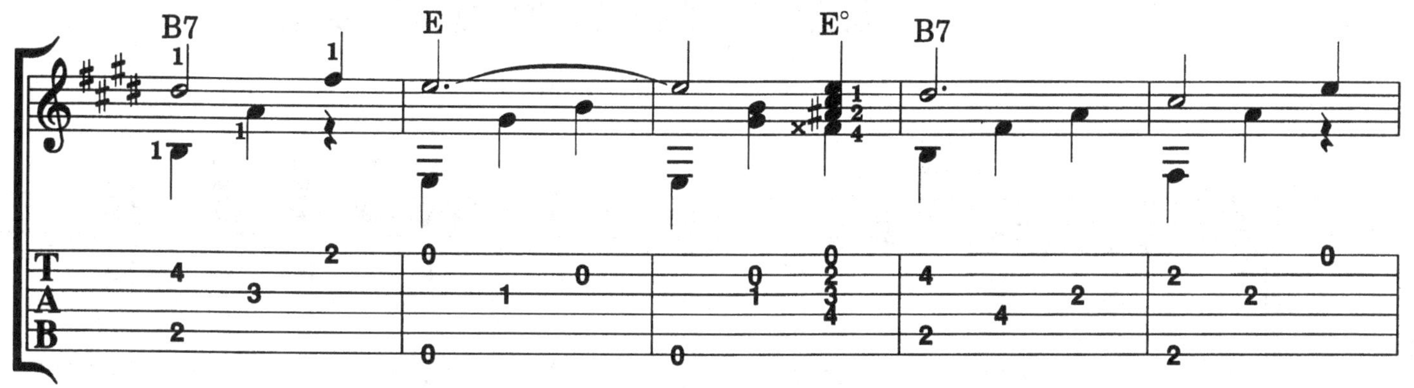
B7
E
E°
B7

E
E°

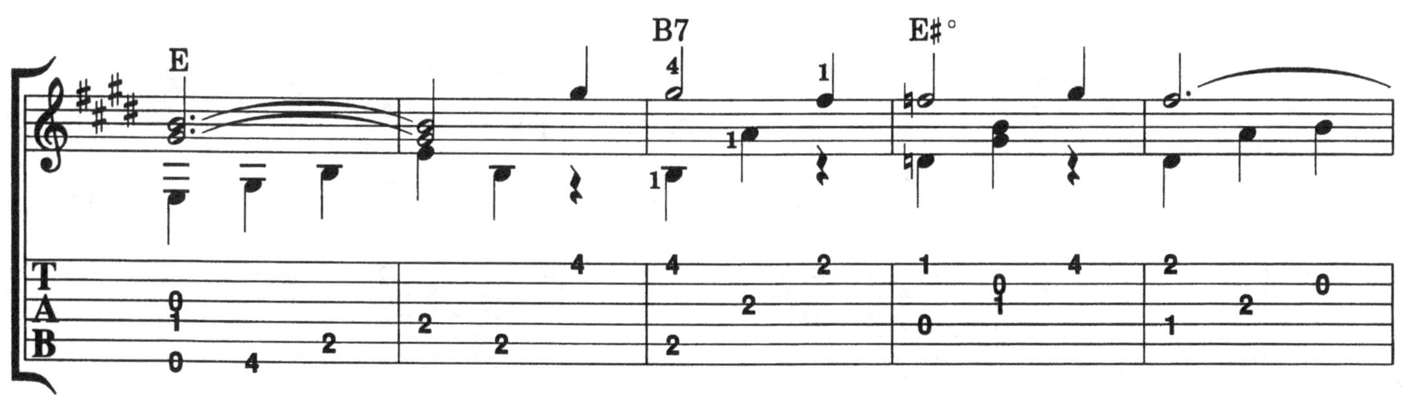
E
B7
E#°

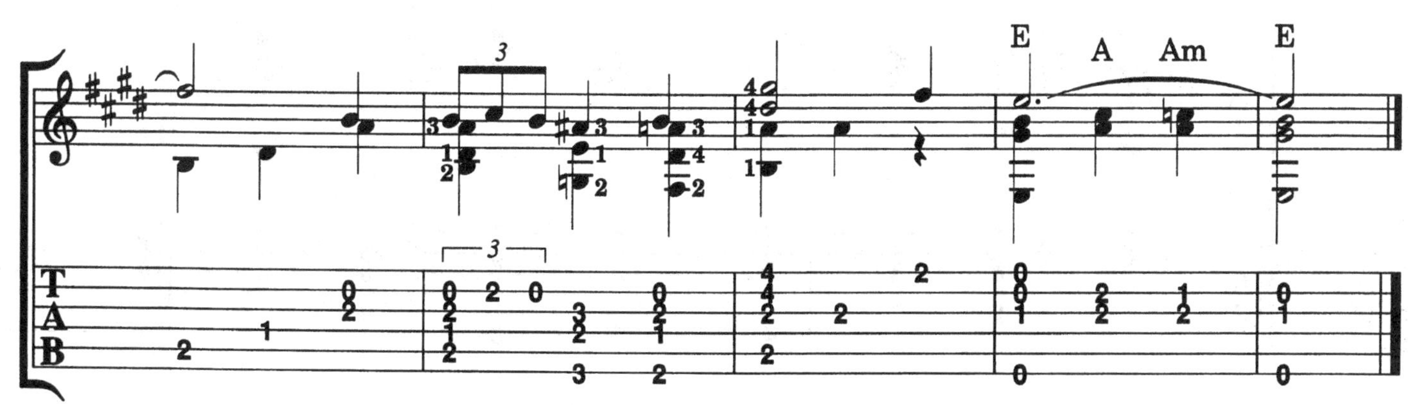
E
A
Am
E

Chopin's Prelude

Spanish Fandango

C
D
G
G
D7*
G
Har.
Slide
D7
Bar V
Bar VII

G
Bar. IV
B
Bar V
C
D Bar. VII
G
Har. 12
Har 7
Har 12
Har.
Har
Har 12
Har 12
Har 7
rit.
Har 5
Har 12.

Just As I Am

Tuning
⑥ ⑤ ④ ③ ② ①
C G D G B E
Classic Guitar

With Expression

The Chords Used in "Just As I Am"

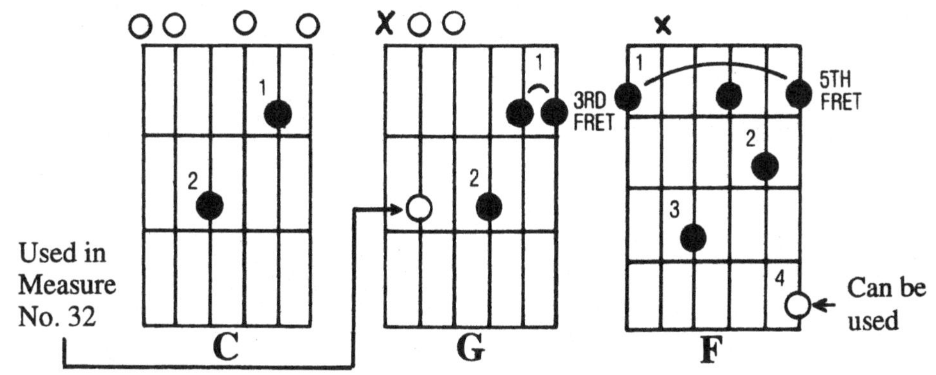

The Chords Used in "John Henry"

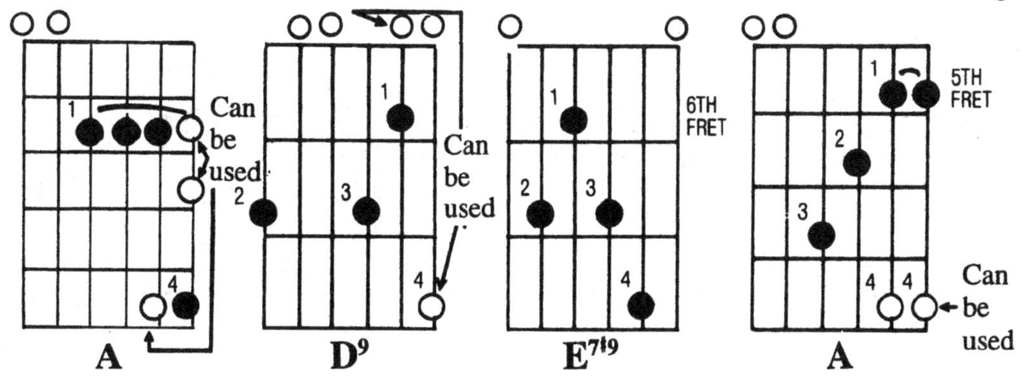

John Henry

Electric Guitar
Muff. Bass

Bright

A D9 A E7(♯9) A D9 A D9 E7♯9 A

Pull off Pull off Bend Pull off Pull off Pull off

* ◡ Bend approximately a quarter tone.

The Chords Used in "Me and Merle"

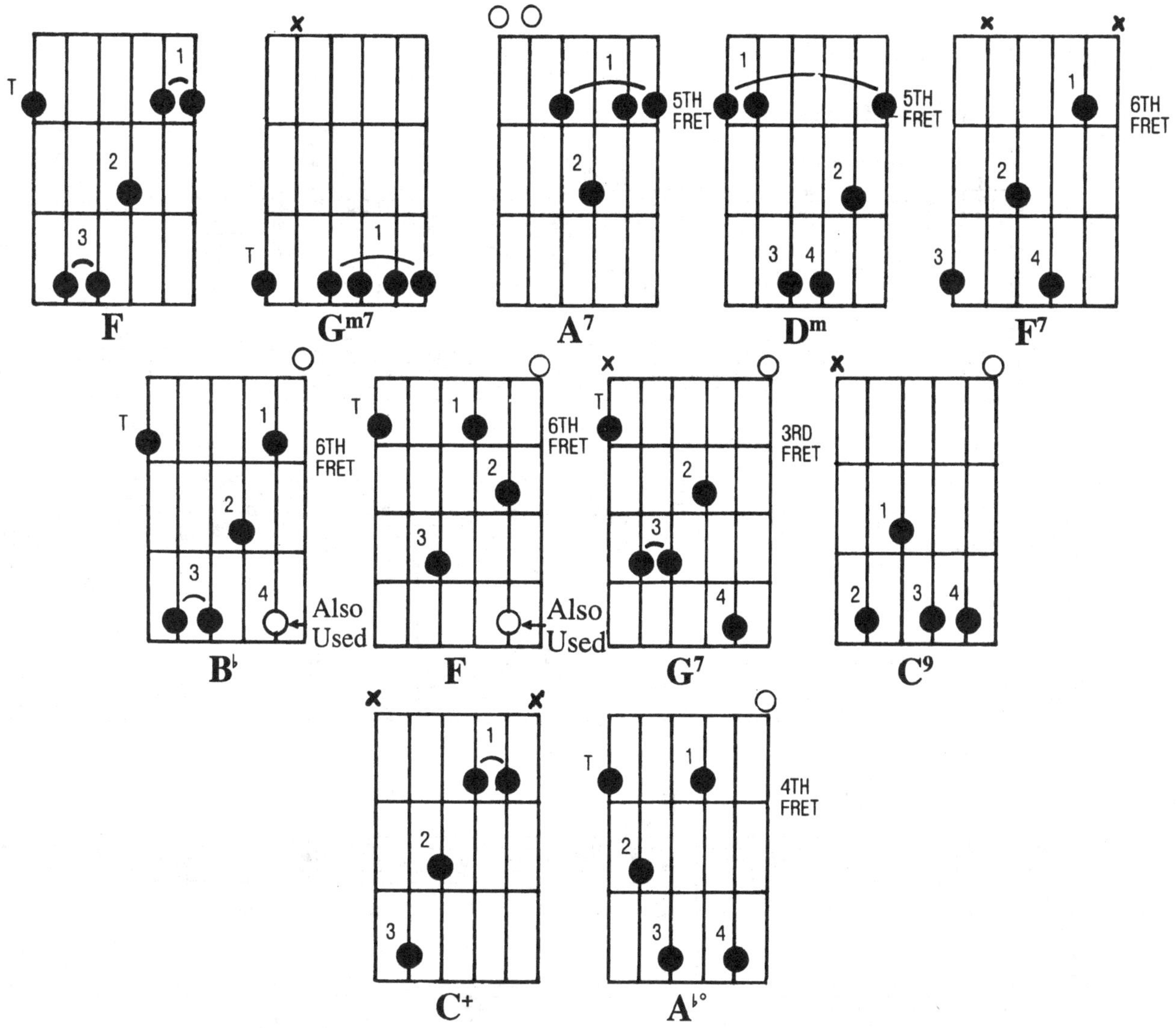

F, Gm7, A7 (5TH FRET), Dm (5TH FRET), F7 (6TH FRET)

B♭ (6TH FRET, Also Used), F (6TH FRET, Also Used), G7 (3RD FRET), C9

C+, A♭° (4TH FRET)

The first string should be played open whenever possible. The object of playing the open E or first string with the F, B♭ and G7 chords is to produce a smoothly flowing legato sound above the steady rhythm of the thumb. Some of the chord changes are anticipated.

A tone is played in advanced of its harmony as in the example below. In the F to G7 change the F or ① string is played before the rhythm changes to G7.

Example

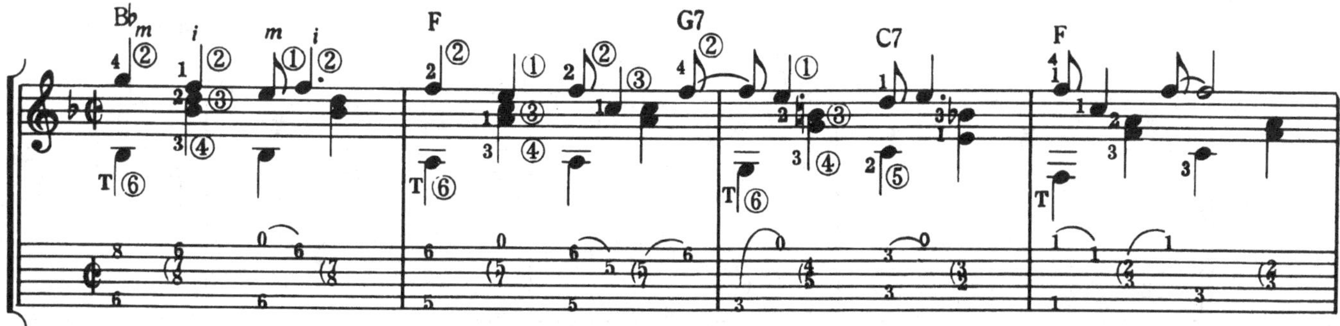

Me and Merle

Electric or Acoustic

By Chet Atkins

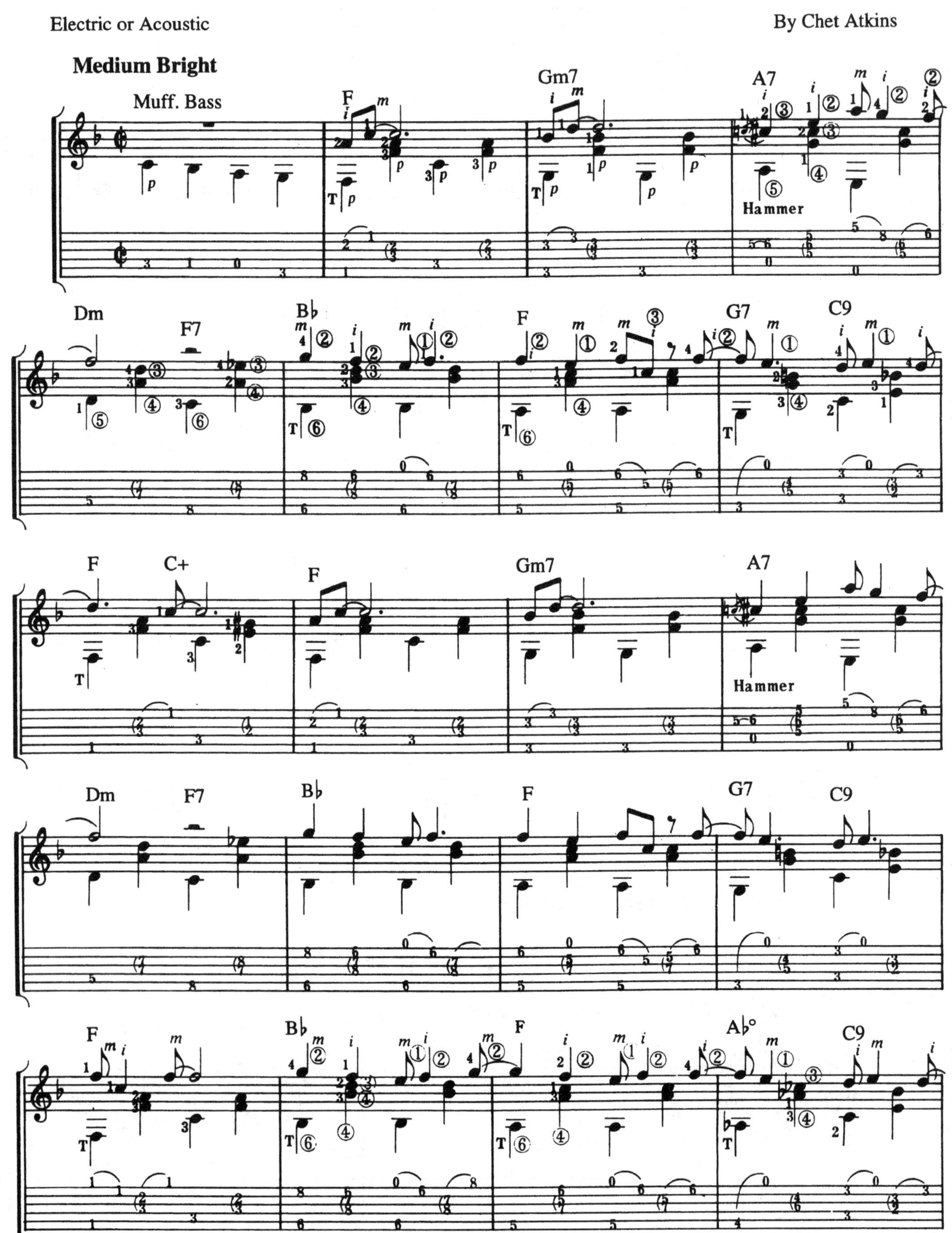

F
B♭
F
G7
C9
F
C+
F
Gm7
A7
Hammer
Dm
F7
B♭
F
G7
C7
F
B♭
F
G7
C7
F
F
Hammer
Pull
off

The Chords Used in "Wimoweh"

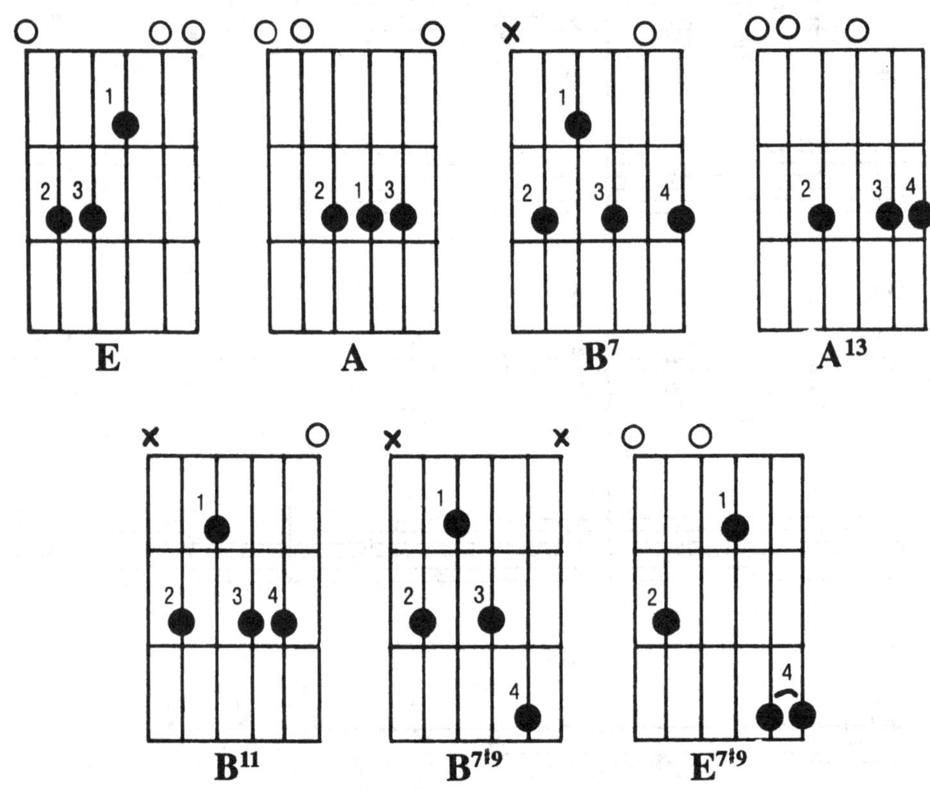

Wimoweh

Electric Guitar

Moderate

E
A
Pull off
E
B7
Pull off
E
A
E
B11
E7
A
E
B7♯9
B7
E
A
E
B7
E
A
Bend 16
E
B7
Bend

* x deaden ⑤ string, use right hand thumb only to pick strings.

The Chords Used in "Liebestraum"

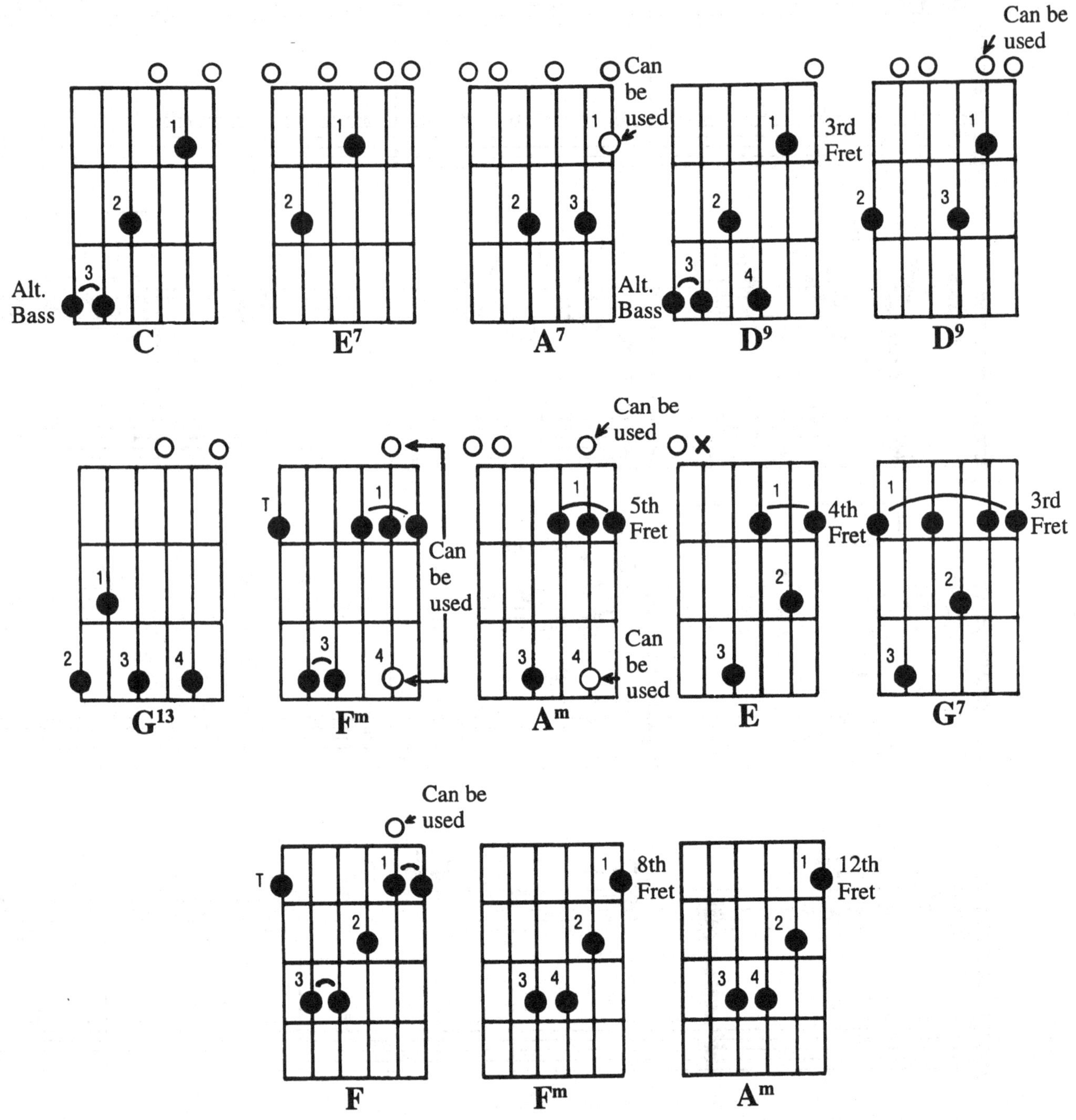

Liebestraum

Classic Guitar

Fm
C
Am
E
G7
C
E7
A7
D9
D9
F
G7
C
p i m

Fm
C
Am
E
G7
C
E7
A7
D7
F
G7
C

⑥string D
Electric Guitar

Czardas

D
Pull off
Em
D
A7
To Coda
D
A7
D
G
legato
E7
Am
Slide
D7

G
Hammer
& Pull off
Hammer
Pull off
Slide
Hammer
Slide
E7
Am
G
half tone
Bend
14 FRET
D7
Bend
½ tone
G
A7
D.S. al Coda
Coda
Repeat 3 times
Repeat 3 times

The Chords Used in "Yankee Doodle Dixie"

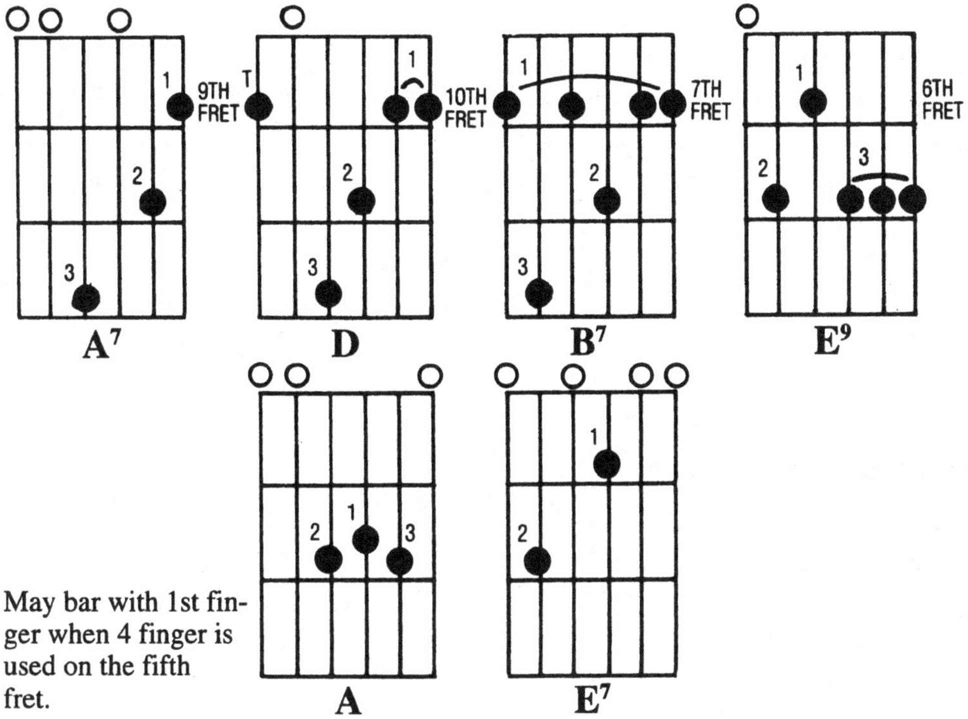

May bar with 1st finger when 4 finger is used on the fifth fret.

The chords are used in the bridge only. The first sixteen measures are actually two melodies played simultaneously and no standard chord forms are used.

Yankee Doodle Dixie

Electric

By Chet Atkins

A7
D
A
E7
A
E7
A
E9
A
A
E7
A
E9
A